The Power
of Blockchain
for Healthcare

The Power of Blockchain for Healthcare

How Blockchain Will Ignite The Future of Healthcare

Ignite Minds.

Capture Value.

Discover Frontiers.

Peter B. Nichol

AUTHOR OF *LEARNING INTELLIGENCE*

For information about permissions to reproduce selections from the book, or about special discounts for bulk purchases, please contact:
booksales@leadersneedpancakes.com

Publisher's Catalog-in-Publication Data
Library of Congress Catalog Card LCCN No. 2017905452

ISBN-13: 978-0692875414
ISBN-10: 0692875417

Printed in the United States of America.

DEDICATION

To all the dreamers who believe we can change the world.
I believe too.

CONTACTING PETER B. NICHOL

The development of this book arose from my passion for healthcare and the belief that each of us holds power to change the world. As an avid writer and contributor to CIO, I wanted to share articles, posts, and my understanding of blockchain within the context of healthcare for the benefit of every leader challenged with making a difference for patients.

The Power of Blockchain for Healthcare is the accumulation and compilation of my recent musings on the tangible impact of blockchain technologies on healthcare.

I welcome your stories, thoughts, and any practical approaches you have to improve applying blockchain to healthcare. I guarantee I'll read all the letters and email I receive. However, due to the pure volume, I'm not able to respond to every request for information.

For leaders, teams, and organizations interested in engaging me for board advisory, consulting, or speaking please contact me at OROCA Innovations:

Peter B. Nichol
Managing Director, OROCA Innovations
145 Barkledge Drive
Newington, CT 06111
E-mail: peter.nichol@orocainnovations.com
Twitter: @peterbnichol

For additional information on the book, *The Power of Blockchain for Healthcare*, please visit the website:
www.leadersneedpancakes.com/blockchainbook

ABOUT THE AUTHOR

PETER B. NICHOL (@peterbnichol) is a business and technology executive, recognized for Digital Innovation by CIO 100, MIT Sloan, Computerworld, and the Project Management Institute. As Managing Director at OROCA Innovations, Peter leads the CXO advisory services practice, driving digital strategies.

Peter was honored as an MIT Sloan CIO Leadership Award Finalist in 2015 and is a regular contributor to CIO.com on innovation. As Head of Information Technology, Peter was responsible for Connecticut's Health Insurance Exchange's (HIX) industry-leading digital platform that transformed consumer and retail-oriented services. Peter championed the Connecticut marketplace digital implementation with a transformational, cloud-based SaaS platform and mobile application and was recognized as a 2014 PMI Project of the Year Award finalist, CIO 100, and received awards for best digital services, API, and platform. He also received a lifetime achievement award for leadership and digital transformation and was honored as a 2016 Computerworld Premier 100 IT Leader.

Peter has a B.S. in Computer Information Systems from Bentley University and an MBA from Quinnipiac University, where he graduated Summa Cum Laude. He earned his Project Management Professional and is a Six Sigma Master Black Belt.

As a Commercial-Rated Aviation Pilot, Yachtsman, and Master Scuba Diver, Peter understands, first hand, how to anticipate change and lead boldly.

"*The Power of Blockchain for Healthcare* presents a crisp and fresh perspective of blockchain tailored to healthcare. Nichol focuses on how blockchain will enhance the patient and provider experience and the technology we use to interaction with patients. A must read!"

— RAJA RAMACHANDRAN

FOUNDER, RIPE.IO AND FORMER MANAGING DIRECTOR, R3CEV

"*The Power of Blockchain for Healthcare* is an essential read for any seasoned leader and with Peter's unique perspectives it's no wonder he is one of the most influential innovation voices onhealthcare innovation. A must read."

— GUILHERME STOCCO

HEAD OF STRATEGY AND INNOVATION AT BANCO ORIGINAL

"Peter offers a new voice presenting fresh perspectives on how blockchain will transform the healthcare experience. *The Power of Blockchain for Healthcare* presents the unconventional potential utilization of blockchain beyond the financial sector and within an industry that is on a verge of a disruption."

— EMILIA POPOSKA

CO-FOUNDER AND CEO, BRONTECH

"Blockchain technology will fundamentally transform, disrupt and change our world much like the internet has done. All industry segments will be affected and it will allow for fundamental shifts in business models. Nichol magnificently articulates the implications for the healthcare industry. A must read for every senior executive whom wants to be prepared for the future."

— JACK SMIES
VICE PRESIDENT & BUSINESS HEAD MIDDLE EAST AT WIPRO

"Peter accelerates past the typical explanation of blockchain, and immediately carves out blockchain's value for healthcare. If you're already familiar with blockchain but truly want to understand how blockchain will disrupt healthcare, then *The Power of Blockchain for Healthcare* is the book for you."

— ERAN ORR
FOUNDER & CEO VRPHYSIO, INC.

"*The Power of Blockchain for Healthcare* provides a compelling argument for the transformative impact that blockchain will have on the patience experience. Nichol magnificently articulates a future vision of health, a vision every executive should experience."

— SAN BANERJEE
HEAD OF CONSUMER DIGITAL SOLUTIONS, HUMANA

PREFACE

Aspiration requires inspiration, and, for inspiration, we need to believe that change is possible. Do you believe? I'm a believer.

It only takes one idea, one mind, or one individual to create an idea that can change the way people think, how they act, and what they value.

I have a secret to share. It's something I've learned over the last several years writing for CIO. It doesn't matter how ground-breaking your idea or how magical it is if no one knows about it. When I was first approached to write this book, I declined. Why would leaders read information in a book they could read elsewhere? They could ask a friend or walk into a bookstore, stopping time as they drifted off into the land of "what-ifs."

However, while presenting on the topic of blockchain in Miami, Florida USA, I polled the audience and posed three questions: (1) Who had read at least one article on blockchain? (2) Who thinks blockchain has value? and (3) Who could explain blockchain to a friend?

What I found was fascinating. About 60 percent of the audience said they had, in fact, read about blockchain, even if it was glancing at the newspaper crammed under a hotel door. Roughly 20 percent said they believed blockchain did have value, but, based on the show of hands, that 20 percent was a bit questionable in their confidence level. Then, lastly, only about five people said they could clearly explain blockchain to a friend.

It was at that moment that something dawned on me: Even the most progressive executives didn't truly understand what blockchain was, why it mattered, or how leaders had applied this foundational technology to impact their business.

Shortly after the conference, I decided I'd design and construct a book to focus on blockchain for healthcare using my articles, posts, and illegible musing as the base of the book to help healthcare leaders better understand blockchain and its impact within the healthcare setting.

I hope you find the structure of this book useful in accelerating your understanding of blockchain, with the noise of technology details largely removed. This isn't a technology book; it's a business book. We won't focus on the nuances and technical detail inherent to blockchain technology. Instead, the intent of this book is to create an overlay of the practical uses for blockchain for healthcare. What can blockchain do? How will it impact our health? Why should you, as a healthcare leader, care?

This book is written for the CXO, the leader, and the innovator that has read a handful of articles and has a basic understanding that blockchain is going to impact the economy but is more interested in how that impact translates into the world of health.

I enjoyed bringing this information together in a way that's not only presentable but will stretch your current thinking. I'll be the first to say that not every application or example provided will be "production ready" by year end. But change is possible if we believe together. The rationale for this book is to crack open existing ideas, stretch your assumptions, and prompt a reflection into the possibilities for a new age of health. Enjoy.

Peter B. Nichol
Connecticut, USA

CONTENTS

ACKNOWLEDGMENTS

*Thank you to the leaders across the world
who shared their time with thousands of discussions
providing inspiration for the book and for the comical
Skype experiences we all shared.*

*A special thank you to
Edward Bukstel and Robert Coli, MD from Clinical
Blockchain, for challenging convention and pushing towards
a better patient experience; William Dailey, MD for his
unique and brilliant perspectives on health and technology;
Jeff Brandt for long evenings reflecting over how to improve
patient experiences; and to the hundreds of innovators and
believers who shared their ideas, stories, and dreams to
achieve better patient outcomes, thank you, our insightful
conversations kept me looking around corners.*

"You have all the reason in the world to achieve your grandest dreams. Imagination plus innovation equals realization."

— DENIS WAITLEY

CHAPTER 1

INTRODUCTION

Are you struggling to understand how blockchain works, why blockchains are secure, or why blockchain technologies will transform the world? Here are brief answers to some common questions about blockchain.

As a healthcare leader in your organization, you have a duty to understand why blockchain technology will transform the economy and how it will impact the patients under your care.

Why Was Blockchain Started?

The bursting of the U.S. housing bubble underpinned the global financial crisis of 2007-08 and caused the value of securities, linked to U.S. real estate, to nosedive. Easy access to subprime loans and the overvaluation of bundled subprime mortgages all leaned on the theory that housing prices would continue to climb.

Ultimately, the Financial Crisis Inquiry Commission determined the entire financial meltdown was avoidable and caused by widespread failures in financial regulation and supervision. There were many reasons for the financial crisis including subprime lending, the growth of the housing bubble, and easy credit conditions. The world believed that "trusted third parties" such as banks and financial institutions were dependable. Unfortunately, the global financial crisis proved intermediaries are fallible. The crisis resulted in evictions, foreclosures, and extended unemployment; it was considered the worst financial crisis since the Great Depression.

In response to this disastrous global financial upheaval, in 2008, Satoshi Nakamoto wrote a paper titled, "Bitcoin: A Peer-to-Peer Electronic Cash System."[1] The paper suggested that trusted third parties could be eliminated from financial transactions.

What's Bitcoin and How Does It Relate to Blockchain?

Bitcoin is a peer-to-peer system for sending payments digitally signed (to the entire Bitcoin network). When the "b" is capitalized, Bitcoin referss to that network, e.g., "I want to understand how the Bitcoin network operates." When the "b" isn't capitalized, the word "bitcoin" is used to describe a unit of account or currency, e.g., "I sent one bitcoin to a friend." The digital signature is made from public keys (given to anyone for sending assets) and private keys (held by the asset owner).

The public ledger of Bitcoin transactions is a technology called a blockchain. Blockchains are permissionless distributed databases or permissionless public records of transactions in chronological order. Blockchain technology creates a decentralized, digital, public record of transactions that's secure, anonymous, tamper-proof, and unchangeable—a shared, single source of truth. Blockchains may be used by any industry where information is transferred and roughly fall into the following six classifications:

1. **Currency:** electronic cash systems without intermediaries
2. **Payment infrastructure:** remittance; sending money in payment
3. **Digital assets:** exchange of information
4. **Digital identity:** IDs for digitally signing to reduce fraud

5. **Verifiable data:** verify the authenticity of information or processes
6. **Smart contracts:** software programs that execute without trusted third parties

How Blockchains Work

For the first time in history, we have a technology—blockchain—that removes or disintermediates the middleman from business transactions and, by doing so, improves the value of existing products, services, and interactions in the following ways:

1. **Preventing double spending:** With blockchain, you can't spend money more than once. Blockchain ensures the authenticity of any asset and prevents duplicate expenditures (real estate, medical claim, insurance, medical device, voting ballot, music and government record or payments to program beneficiaries).
2. **Establishing consensus:** In this new model, "crowds" are networks of computers that work together to reach an agreement. Once 51% of the computers in the network agree, "consensus" has been reached and the transaction is recorded in the blockchain—the digital ledger. The blockchain contains an infinite, ordered list of transactions. Each computer contains a full copy of the entire blockchain ledger. Therefore, if one computer attempts to submit an invalid transaction, the computers in the network won't reach consensus (51% agreement), and the transaction won't be added to the blockchain.

There are four principles of permissionless blockchain networks:

1. **Distributed:** The blockchain is decentralized and spread across all the peers participating in the

network. Every computer (full node) has a copy of
the blockchain.

2. **Public:** The actors in a blockchain transaction are
    hidden, but everyone can see all transactions.
3. **Time-stamped:** The dates and times of all transac-
    tions are recorded in plain view.
4. **Persistent:** Because of consensus and the digital
    record, blockchain transactions can't catch fire, be
    misplaced, or become damaged by water.

Steps to create a block (transaction)

Blocks are a record of transactions, and chains are a series of
connected transactions (blocks).

1. **Create transaction:** A miner (computer) creates a
    block.
2. **Solve the puzzle:** A miner must do mathematical
    calculations and, if correct, will receive a "proof of
    work."
3. **Receive proof of work:** If the puzzle is solved—a
    proof of work is issued. The proof of work is a piece
    of data that's difficult (costly, time-consuming) to
    produce but easy for others to verify and which
    satisfies certain requirements. In short, it's difficult
    to solve the puzzle but easy to verify if it's solved
    correctly.
4. **Broadcast proof of work:** The miner broadcasts its
    successful proof of work to other miners.
5. **Verification:** Other miners verify the proof of work.
6. **Publish block:** If 51% of the miners agree (achieve
    consensus) that the proof presented by the miner
    solved the puzzle, that transaction is published to the
    blockchain.

Why Are Blockchains Secure?

With blockchain technologies, truth can also be measured, and consumers and producers can prove data is authentic and uncompromised.

To create a new block—which we'll call block 101—some of the data is used (or a hash is created by an algorithm that turns an arbitrarily large amount of data into a fixed-length random number) from the previous block, block 100. To create block 102, information from block 101 is used, and so on.

Each transaction is dependent on the prior transaction, similar to a light string on a Christmas tree. If a light bulb were pulled from the string (changing a transaction), the miner would have to change every previous transaction ever made in that string (change one light bulb, change them all after that bulb). Probabilistically, this is almost impossible, as not every proposed change would result in consensus.

The result is an immutable digital record for every agreed transaction: a single source of truth.

Why Blockchain Technologies Will Transform the World

Blockchain technologies will improve trust in industries where information (assets) is transferred, including these:

1. **Accounting:** auditing and fraud prevention
2. **Aerospace:** location of parts and chain-of-custody
3. **Energy:** smart metering and decentralized energy grid
4. **Healthcare:** medical devices and health information interoperability
5. **Finance:** remittance and currency exchange
6. **Real-estate:** deeds transfer and accelerated buying or selling of property
7. **Education:** better management of assessments, credentials, transcripts

The blockchain is more than cryptocurrency, and blockchain is not Bitcoin. Blockchain provides a distributed, public, time-stamped, and persistent record of transactions.

BUSINESS MODEL DISRUPTION

Blockchain changes business models and will affect everything from the clothes you wear to the food you eat and even the products you buy.

The customer experience—as your company understands it—is transforming. Your organization might not even realize there's a new revolution coming at you—the blockchain revolution.

Blockchain will have enormous impacts on global business and the world economy. This tectonic shift will disrupt your consumers and change their behavior. Blockchain technology will be injected into everything.

There's a great divide between the technologist that wants to talk about protocols and argue the benefits of state channels and the business technology executive who's eager to understand how blockchain's technology can be applied to the business of healthcare in practical terms. For now, we'll be on the side of the practical business leader; later we'll drift into the theoretical to pontificate what's around the corner.

IMPORTANCE OF CONSENSUS

One of the many papers submitted to the Office of the National Coordinator for Health IT (ONC) Blockchain Challenge was titled, "Co-Creation of Trust for Healthcare: The Cryptocitizen Framework for Interoperability With Blockchain," which I co-authored with Jeff Brandt, an expert in mobility, security, and healthcare.

The paper explains the blockchain trust framework for healthcare by first clarifying the theory behind consensus and cryptocitizens. Here's an excerpt:

To conceptualize the different types of trust ecosystems, we draw on two theoretical foundations: consensus and cryptocitizen.[2]

Discovered by the Portuguese in 1527 and lying about nine degrees north of the equator, the 39-square-mile island of Yap is the most western of the Caroline Islands, which are part of the Federated States of Micronesia located in the Pacific Ocean. William Henry Furness visited the island in 1903 and wrote about the island's stone money in his book titled, The Island of Stone Money UAP of The Carolines, published in 1910. The Yapese did not use money; their medium of exchange was called fei. These large 'coins' were stone wheels ranging from one foot to twelve feet, with a hole in the center, where a pole could be inserted for transportation. The rai stones could weigh up to 8,800 lbs. As a result, it was not always practical to transfer the stone physically from the seller to the buyer for payment. Therefore, the community would communicate at the council square in the center of the village where all the chiefs met when discussing the affairs of the tribe. Here it would be agreed that a transfer was being made from family A to family B. Additionally, because of the weight of the rai stones, typically eight strong men were needed to move the stones, in a sense, building community consensus for the ownership transfer.[3]

The paper elaborates on the value of consensus and how ownership is administered in a healthcare setting. The island of Yap provides a clear example of consensus without technology. It's with this understanding that we, as innovators, can gain a better sense of why consensus matters and how it could be extended into the digital world.

Value of Blockchain

The blockchain is hard to understand, so let's provide a societal example to illustrate how blockchain will impact finance and humanity.

Traditional financial auditing as we know it has ended. Financial auditing will experience the most extreme business model change since the passage of the Sarbanes-Oxley Act (SOX) in 2002. New financial auditing with blockchain ensures that businesses are fiscally responsible. This business model change will save lives.

On January 10, 2010, a 7.0-magnitude earthquake with an epicenter 16 miles from Haiti's capital, Port-au-Prince, ripped through the country, followed by more than 52 aftershocks measuring 4.5 magnitude or greater. The Red Cross received $488 million in donations to help the Haitian population, yet, somehow, according to CNN, the Red Cross only built six permanent homes. A year later, the death toll was estimated at between 160,000 and 300,000.[4]

The Red Cross repeatedly declined to disclose how donations were distributed for Haitian relief. It's safe to say that, despite almost $500 million raised, disaster victims did not receive all donated funds. Haiti is a classic example of the controversy over transparency.

RUBIX TEAM TAKES A SWING AT FRAUD

At the 2016 Shanghai Blockchain Hackathon, the Deloitte Rubix Team launched a new solution called PermaRec (permanent record) during this two-day event. Jennifer Qin Yi, an audit partner of Deloitte Beijing and the lead partner responsible for the coordination of Deloitte's investment management industry in Asia Pacific, led the team. Deloitte's solution allows companies to record transactions in a globally distributed ledger residing on the blockchain.

The Deloitte PermaRec solution connects SAP, Oracle, and other financial reporting systems, enabling Deloitte to review transactions from both parties to ensure legitimacy and appease regulators. While the product isn't mature, the thinking is nothing short of visionary.

What if this PermaRec solution had been available to the Red Cross in 2010? It's more than likely that many Haitian lives would have been saved. As a result of blockchain, the business of donations to support disaster relief will dramatically change.

When consumers must decide between donating disaster-relief funds to an organization where every transaction is publically available on a blockchain or to an organization that doesn't share donation disbursement details—the decision will be quick. The business of charity has just changed.

BLOCKCHAIN CHANGES BUSINESS MODELS

The Association of Certified Fraud Examiners (ACFE) estimates that fraud costs organizations worldwide $3.7 trillion a year or 5 percent of the Gross World Product (GWP).[5] By extending blockchain to this application, we can tackle fraud. In the case of Medicaid, Medicare, and Social Security, fraud could be impacted by conducting transactions to beneficiaries and providers serviced from the blockchain.

Blockchains can be used in any situation when a verifiable public record is required, and blockchain benefits from not being under the control of any one entity.

Blockchain technology, when applied to healthcare, has the potential to decrease corruption and fraud, creating entirely new business models.

Before you hear about the real benefits and value of blockchain, you first must muster through the hype surrounding it. Let's clear that up now.

Predicting Innovations: Deciding When to Move

The pitted history of innovation is fraught with bad information, poor advice, and unstable experts—from the overly enthusiastic to the sorely pessimistic—so we must listen for a balanced tone. One expert is right. One expert is wrong.

How accurate are predictions?[6] Every day, we have plans, even if that plan is to do nothing. At some point, knowing what the weather might be becomes a factor in the decision about what to do, where to go, or what to wear. A product manager at Minitab answered a question we've wondered about. How accurate are those weather forecasters?"

There are three main forecast periods: 10-day, five-day, and next-day. The Minitab manager's experiment recorded 10-day, five-day, and next-day weather forecasts. Over 30 days, the rolling forecast and the actual weather was recorded. For some days, the forecasts were more accurate than others. Not surprising, the 10-day forecast was less accurate than the five-day forecast, and the five-day was less accurate than the next-day forecast. As the prediction date moved closer to the actual date, less variability was observed in the prediction.

Usually, we talk about the standard deviation of defects, whether in the technological or manufacturing space.[7] However, in this case, we're talking about the extent to which one weather forecaster agreed with another. Do experts mostly agree or mostly disagree? A low standard deviation isn't always good, and a high isn't always bad. Standard deviation is a factor of the observation data spread—in this case, how close one weather forecaster was to another in their predictions of the actual weather.

The standard deviations varied based on the forecast period. The 10-day forecast had a standard deviation of 6.2 degrees, with the high temp off as much as 8 degrees and the low temp off by as much as 17 degrees. The standard deviations of the five-day forecast (4.3 degrees) and the next-day forecast (2.1 degrees) were less pronounced.

Does any of this even matter? What if we weren't talking about weather forecasters? What if we were talking about experts predicting the lack of impact of blockchain on business or experts predicting the impact of new innovative technologies? Think about the business impact of blockchain in 10 years, five years, and one year.

Brilliant Innovations or Dreadful Embarrassments?

The prediction depends on which expert you ask. Television, radio, telephone, transportation, computers, space exploration, and medicine are riddled with renowned experts who've offered dire predictions. The most humorous were the most pessimistic. Keep that in mind when you hear experts offer ridiculously pessimistic outlooks on the impact of blockchain technologies on the business, the economy, and the world.

The following are examples of very wrong predictions about innovative and transformative technologies.

TELEVISION

"Television won't be able to hold on to any market it captures after the first six months. People will soon get tired of staring at a plywood box every night."
– Darryl F. Zanuck, Head of 20th-Century Fox, 1946.

20th-Century Fox entered the television broadcasting arena in 1949 with shows on ABC and CBS and later evolved into the Fox Television Network.

RADIO

"Radio has no future."
– Lord Kelvin, British mathematician, and physicist, ca. 1897

As of Oct. 22, 2016, the market capitalization of Sirius XM Holdings was $20.2 billion.

TELEPHONE

> "This 'telephone' has too many shortcomings to be serious-
> ly considered as a practical form of communication. The
> device inherently is of no value to us."
> – Western Union internal memo, 1878

Verizon, the largest player in the wireless market, saw an operating income margin of 33.5 percent for FY 2016 on reve-
nues of $125.9 billion—not bad for a market that is of "no
value."[8]

TRANSPORTATION

> "What can be more palpably absurd than the prospect held
> out of locomotives traveling twice as fast as stagecoaches?"
> – The Quarterly Review, England, 1825

Yahoo Finance reports that the market capitalization of the
railway industry was $317,948 billion in 2016.

COMPUTERS

> "There is no reason anyone would want a computer in their
> home."
> – Ken Olson, president, chairman, and founder of Digital
> Equipment Corp., 1977

The personal computer industry is about $24 billion, not bad
considering that smartphones have shifted the PC market.
Adding smartphones (iPhone, Android) dramatically increases the growth estimates. Global revenue from smartphones
climbed to $428.9 billion in full-year 2016.[9]

SPACE EXPLORATION

"There is no hope for the fanciful idea of reaching the moon because of insurmountable barriers to escaping the Earth's gravity."
– Dr. Forest Ray Moulton, University of Chicago astronomer, 1932

In 1959, the Soviet Union made the first spacecraft landings on the lunar surface with Luna 2 and Luna 3. [10][11] The United States reached the moon in 1964 and 1965 with Ranger 7 and Ranger 8.[12][13]

MEDICINE

"The abdomen, the chest and the brain will forever be shut from the intrusion of the wise and humane surgeon."
– Sir John Eric Ericson, Surgeon to Queen Victoria, 1873

In 1967, a South African physician, Dr. Christiaan Barnard, performed the world's first human-to-human heart transplant at Groote Schuur Hospital, Cape Town.[14]

What did the individuals making these predictions have in common? They were all among the most renowned industry experts of their times, and each offered horrible advice. It's comical to think about the big innovations of 100 to 200 years ago that were ignored or dismissed by experts.

What are the innovations in experimentation today that experts have dismissed? Tesla? Airbnb? Next-generation sequencing (NGS)? VR headsets (sports, shopping, therapy)? Blockchain?

The Hype of Blockchain Uncovered: Beyond the Hype

To absorb the massive virality and impact of the blockchain, we must first address the hype. Hype, please square up. The premise that blockchain is hype is false.

What is hype? The Oxford Dictionary defines hype as, "promoting or publicizing (a product or idea) intensively, often exaggerating its importance or benefits." The simple version is that hype is an exaggerated advantage—a benefit that doesn't align with the future reality of the product or service. As with many new technologies, there's excitement. However, the buzz and excitement around blockchain are more than hype; it's the realization of the potential to transform industries.

MEDIA WEIGHS IN

Thought leaders from Forbes and Harvard Business Review have bought into the value of blockchain technologies. For example, Jerry Cuomo, an IBM Fellow and Forbes contributor, in his February 2016 Forbes article, "Blockchain: The Foundation For The Future Of Transactions," stated that "Blockchain has the potential to become the technological foundation for all electronic transactions conducted over the Internet."[15] Amy Webb, in her January 2015 Harvard Business Review article titled, "The Tech Trends You Can't Ignore In 2015" stated, "Even if Bitcoin itself never really gains traction, blockchain technology has enormous promise."[16]

INDUSTRY JOINS THE PARTY

It's great that the media has received the mailer on the value of blockchain, but what about the industry?

CISCO recently stated, "The next generation of the Internet is coming with Blockchain."[17] In February of this year, Accenture launched a blockchain practice for the financial services industry and announced blockchain partnerships with Broadridge, and PwC, showcasing that the "new practice will implement emerging technology that is projected to reduce financial services industry costs by more than $20 billion annually by

2021." PwC, on April 4, 2016, announced it has started a new global technology team to tap into blockchain and has recruited 15 new leading technology and business specialists.[18]

Deloitte has predicted the tipping point of blockchain won't arrive until 2027. In a recent report titled, "Blockchain. Enigma. Paradox. Opportunity," Deloitte stated, "Ultimately, the blockchain is not just about cryptocurrencies and faster peer-to-peer payments."[19] On October 2015, Deloitte partnered with Colu to bring the startup into new global markets. Colu allows users to issue and track their digital assets on its platform.

The industry is unifying and joining the blockchain revolution. R3 (R3CEV LLC) leads a consortium consisting of 43 financial companies in the research and development of blockchain usage in the financial system. Todd McDonald, co-founder, and head of strategy for R3, likely wouldn't refer to blockchain as hype, either.

The world has taken notice of blockchain.

HISTORICAL PERSPECTIVES ON INNOVATION HYPE

The fact that, through early 2017, large investors poured over $1.55 billion into blockchain technology doesn't persuade some colonialists.[20]

Remember the hype over the telephone in the nineteenth century? The telephone has matured, but has the hype? We all know how overstated the future of the telephone was by the end of the nineteenth and start of the twentieth centuries. How about the buzz and overpromises about canals and railroads in the 1700s and 1800s? Hype probably isn't the best word to describe the development of railroads, which was one of the most important phenomena of the Industrial Revolution.

The list doesn't seem to end and continues with the likes of automobiles and radios and then the jet engine, rockets, and atomic energy and on into the 1950s and 1960s with biotechnology, nanotechnology, and genomics.

Do we consider the impact of canals, railroads, telephones, automobiles, and cell phones hype? If these hyped technologies landed us here, imagine how blockchain can change society in the future.

Hype Cycle

The Gartner Hype Cycle, introduced in 1995, offers useful insights into the promise of emerging technology. The July 2015 "Gartner Hype Cycle for Emerging Technologies" report highlighted the phases of the hype cycle in emerging and collaborative tech.

The five phases of the Hype Cycle are: innovation trigger (less than 2 years), peak of inflated expectations (2 to 5 years), trough of disillusionment (5 to 10 years), slope of enlightenment (more than a decade), and, lastly, the plateau of productivity (obsolesce might occur before the plateau). It could be argued that the Hype Cycle isn't a cycle, that outcomes don't depend on the nature of the technology itself, or that it's less than scientific in nature because it doesn't account for changes over time to the speed at which technology develops. However, it does effectively show how society feels about new technology and when historically inflated expectations and disenchantments should likely occur.

CLOUD HYPE CYCLE

If we consider Cloud started its innovation trigger phase in 2012, the phases of the Cloud hype cycle would be the following:

1. **Innovation trigger** (2012 to 2013)
2. **Peak of inflated expectations** (2014 to 2018)
3. **Trough of disillusionment** (2019 to 2028)
4. **Slope of enlightenment** (beginning 2030)
5. **The plateau of productivity** (if applicable, after 2028)

BLOCKCHAIN HYPE CYCLE

If we consider blockchain's innovation trigger phase started in 2014—based on when serious investors began to weigh in—the phases of the blockchain hype cycle would be the following:

1. **Innovation trigger** (2014 to 2015)
2. **Peak of inflated expectations** (2016 to 2020)
3. **Trough of disillusionment** (2021 to 2030)
4. **Slope of enlightenment** (beginning 2030)
5. **The plateau of productivity** (if applicable, after 2030)

The charts below illustrate the phases of the Hype Cycle, showing visibility and expectations over time. If you're looking for additional sources on the Hype Cycle, Jackie Fenn and Mark Raskino have an excellent book titled, *Mastering the Hype Cycle: How to Choose the Right Innovation at the Right Time.*[21]

Beyond Finance

Returning to the Satoshi Nakamoto paper mentioned at the outset of this chapter, "Bitcoin: A Peer-to-Peer Electronic Cash System," if what's presented in this paper is the only framework used to evaluate blockchain, that would be a narrow view of its potential. Minimizing the value of blockchain would be akin to stating, in 1995, that the Internet would be used just for email.

Blockchain is much more than cryptocurrency, and the benefits of blockchain will extend well beyond financial markets. For example, healthcare is ripe for disruption and applications of blockchain may include:

1. **Smart property:** prescription drugs and regulated pharmaceuticals
2. **Smart contracts between payer, provider, and doctor:** decreased fraud and reimbursement

3. **eBay-type bidding for medical services:** discrete and anonymized
4. **Health databanks:** universal medical records, personal genomics

Similar to the Internet in 1995, we don't know where blockchain will go. The one thing we do know is it's not just hype.

A quote that captures well the sentiment surrounding blockchain is from Bill Gates, a technologist and philanthropist, in which he states, "We always overestimate the change that will occur in the next two years and underestimate the change that will occur in the next ten. Don't let yourself be lulled into inaction."

"No matter what people tell you, words and ideas can change the world."

— ROBIN WILLIAMS

CHAPTER 2

IDEAS THAT BEND CONVENTION

L et me guess: you thought blockchains were immutable. We'll explore the mystery behind breaking the blockchain. What does this all mean for business? You thought blockchains were distributed, public, time-stamped, and persistent. Guess what. They still are.

Permissionless or Permissioned Blockchains?

The financial crisis of 2007-08 wasn't solved with a $700-billion bailout. Forbes correctly stated that the special inspector general for the Troubled Asset Relief Program (TARP) summarized the total government bailout commitment at $16.8 trillion dollars, with $4.6 trillion already paid out as of 2015.[1]

Fast-forward eight years, and Wells Fargo—previously a respected financial services firm—on Sept. 8, 2016, agreed to a $185-million settlement with the Consumer Financial Protection Bureau, the Office of the Comptroller of the Currency, and the Los Angeles city attorney.[2] Over two million fake bank accounts had been created, and Wells Fargo fired 5,300 employees during the period under investigation.

It doesn't seem that long ago that, in 2008, Satoshi Nakamoto spoke of the ability to transfer cash electronically, peer-to-peer, to avoid "trusted third parties." Trusted third parties can be eliminated from financial transactions in a permission-less blockchain.

A permissioned blockchain depends on "trusting" entities. Lehman Brothers, AIG, Citigroup, Countrywide, and JPMorgan were all trusted third parties in 2006 and all untrusted by 2007. In 2012, Wells Fargo was a trusted thirty party. By 2016—untrusted. Faith in trusted third parties is waning. The public is growing tired of self-created trust.

Does a need exist for information in a blockchain to be deleted and not just append-only, or is this model designed to fail? How is trust established in this imperfect world?

Private Blockchains Introduce a Trusted Intermediary

Accenture suggested that permissioned blockchains will benefit from the ability to change transactions—i.e., perform "do-overs."

A permissioned blockchain is a network where the participants can restrict who can participate in the consensus mechanism of the blockchain's network. In other words, it's a network where the trusted entities or companies self-elect themselves as trustworthy. Who monitors them? They monitor themselves—at least that's the theory.

REMOVING THE MYSTERIOUS INNOVATION CURTAIN

Undeniable signatures to practical privacy and chameleon signatures to redactable blockchains—who's behind the innovation of editing the blockchain? Accenture or IBM?

Four academics—Giuseppe Ateniese (USA), Bernardo Magri (Italy), Daniele Venturi (Italy), and Ewerton Andrade (Brazil) (referenced as AMVE here onward)—are the inventors behind the new framework to rewrite and or compress the content of blocks. Their joint paper, "Redactable Blockchain, or Rewriting History in Bitcoin and Friends," published Aug. 5, 2016, expands on the early IBM Watson Chameleon Signatures research published in 2000.[34]

Hugo Krawczyk and Tal Rabin were both IBM researchers and drafted Chameleon Signatures in 2000. They introduced these signatures to provide an undeniable commitment of the signer to the contents of a signed document. The enhancement over digital signatures is that the new signature did "not allow the recipient of the signature to disclose the substance of the signed information to any third party without the signers' consent."

REFRESH ME, WHERE DID THIS ALL START?

Zero-knowledge proofs remain the foundation of Undeniable Signatures, a digital signature scheme and implementation presented by David Chaum and Hans van Antwerpen in 1989.[5] In January 1992, Jurjen Bos wrote his dissertation, "Practical Privacy," on control coding theories, measurement, and cryptology.[6]

This thesis laid the foundation for a paper that appeared in *Advances in Cryptology—CRYPTO '92* titled, "Provably Unforgeable Signatures," published in 2001.[7] Provably Unforgeable Signatures improved on existing schemes by offering signatures that were smaller, so signing and verification required less memory and computing power.

A REDACTABLE BLOCKCHAIN

Accenture recently released its most articulate blockchain paper to date, called "Editing the Uneditable Blockchain: Why Distributed Ledger Technology Must Adapt to an Imperfect World," which is apparently based on the primary work, "Redactable Blockchain, or Rewriting History in Bitcoin and Friends."[8][9]

Since 2009, there have been 210.2 million bitcoin transactions.[10] None of those transactions have been removed, redacted, or rewritten. They were and continue to be immutable.

Does removing the immutability of blockchains address human error? During our MIT CIO Symposium discussion, "How Blockchain Will Transform the Digital Economy," my colleague Anders Brownworth of Circle suggested private or permissioned blockchains were equivalent to an intranet—cosmetic and functionless.[11] I agree.

IS THERE A DIFFERENCE BETWEEN A CONSORTIUM OPERATING A PRIVATE BLOCKCHAIN AND A CARTEL?

Private blockchains aren't required to protect intellectual property or privacy. Smart contracts with private code can do this. If you had to choose between banking at a nonprofit bank operating on a public blockchain with smart contracts or banking at a for-profit bank operating on a private blockchain, where would you bank?

The pragmatists believe peer-to-peer trust is possible. Idealists clutch onto the world unchanged, controlled by a self-selected minority.

Creating a Blockchain Undo Button

Leaked encryption keys, offensive material, and errors—as in the case of a medical records—suggest that editable blockchains are worth reflection.

Situations exist where the ability to go back in time and perform an "undo" appear to make sense. In these contexts, we imagine a fair and balanced world operating in harmony—a utopian version of the modern Internet of Things.

THE STRUGGLE FOR FREEDOM OF EXPRESSION

Censorship has been explained as actions taken in the best interests of the public. A benevolent public concern for morality. China's censorship of WeChat for example.[12] The decision by India's film censor to cut 94 scenes from a movie about Punjab's drug problem.[13] Michelangelo's 1565 "The Last Judgement."[14]

Freedom of speech is the right to articulate one's opinions and ideas without fear of government retaliation or censorship, or societal sanction—the right to be heard.

Does a network hold trust if all voices aren't heard? Are we still talking about the ability to edit a transaction or present proof-of-trust, or provide immutability?

The concepts of freedom of speech and trust aren't mutually exclusive.

WHAT IS A REDACTABLE BLOCKCHAIN?

According to AMVE, a blockchain is editable by adding a link to each link of the hash chain. Think of each block-to-block link as a lock (physical lock) in which a key is required to unlock it. In a permissionless blockchain, there's no key, making the series of transactions or blocks immutable. In a permissioned blockchain, this "trapdoor key" can be given to miners, a centralized auditor, or shares of the key can be distributed among several authorities. In this context, these operators will have the ability to repair blocks, e.g., blocks can be deleted, modified, or inserted into existing blocks.

THE ARGUMENT SUPPORTING AN EDITABLE BLOCKCHAIN

The authors of the editable blockchain concept developed in "Redactable Blockchain, or Rewriting History in Bitcoin and Friends" come from varied academic backgrounds. Giuseppe Ateniese is a professor in and director of the computer science department at the Stevens Institute of Technology. Bernardo Magri is a researcher at the Sapienza University of Rome. Daniele Venturi is an assistant professor at the University of Trento. Ewerton Andrade is a researcher at the University of São Paulo.

I had the good fortune to speak with Bernardo Magri, one of the visionary authors behind the editable blockchain concept. Magri conducts research on both the theoretical and practical aspects of cryptography.

He joked, "Working with cryptocurrencies is a shot in the dark, as the community's reaction to the work can be completely unpredictable—you never know if they will love your work or hate it." It's fair to say the industry loved the work on redactable blockchains.

Magri said there's one thing the public often gets wrong: "The public has trouble understanding the inner workings of blockchain technology. Therefore, it's normal that they also have trouble seeing the benefits of this technology, over a simple centralized database system. Adding a redactable feature to a blockchain, does not make it centralized at all. The blockchain will continue to operate as usual, and depending on how the chameleon hash is shared the trust assumption could remain the same." Redactable blockchains are possible when the trusted entities are limited (a variation of M-of-N multisig).

Do we need a blockchain with a delete button? AMVE identified two industry approaches for the facilitation of the blockchain technology to implement decentralized services and applications: (1) an overlay on top of Bitcoin and (2) the creation of an alternative blockchain.

There are four motivations supporting the desirability of redactable blockchains.

1. **Abuse:** the ability to correct the storage of arbitrary messages, e.g., Bitcoin has already been abused by offensive material cemented into its walls for eternity.

2. **Rewritable storage:** classic blockchains don't scale and waste precious resources. Rewriting presents new storage options, e.g., CD-R.

3. **Inability to expunge:** permitting the deletion of records, if required, e.g., in case they contain errors (medical records), sensitive information when it's necessary by law, or if personal encryption keys are leaked.

4. **Inter-entity interactions:** consolidation is difficult to achieve with immutable blockchains, e.g., this removes the impossibility of consolidating past transactions without affecting any subsequent blocks. This feature is necessary to combine distinct accounting structures, budgets, or transactions.

ADAPTING THE FRAMEWORK TO THE TYPES OF BLOCKCHAINS

AMVE anticipated the next logical question: How are keys managed across the three main types of real-world blockchains?

⟩ Redact

1. **Private blockchain:** the ability to write is bestowed upon a central authority. This example is straightforward, with the "trapdoor key" given to a central authority having the power to compute collisions and, therefore, redact blocks. A single operator has the power to redact.

2. **Consortium blockchain:** consensus is predetermined by a finite group of parties. In this example, the "trapdoor key" is shared among consortium parties and redactions can be made through secure, multiparty computation (MPC) protocols similar to M-of-N multisigs (where multiple consortium parties grant the redaction before authorization is approved). A select few have the power to redact.

Shared ✓

3. **Public blockchain:** decentralized with no central operator, and any party can submit transactions to the network, e.g., a permissionless blockchain such as Bitcoin. AMVE offers two suggestions for this type of blockchain: (a) distribute the "trapdoor" to all parties using multiparty computation (MPC) protocols; and (b) distribute to a chosen subset of parties. Suggestion b implied that all parties have equal power to redact. However, the top seven mining pools in Bitcoin already control 70 percent of the total network hashing power.

Permission

What Happens If There Are HIPAA Violations?

The Health Insurance Portability and Accountability Act of 1996 (HIPAA) is United States legislation that provided data privacy and security provisions for safeguarding medical information. There are many HIPAA violations that can occur. Below are 10 of the most common violations:

- **Lost or stolen devices,** e.g., unencrypted computer loss
- **Unauthorized access,** e.g., database breaches or employees illegally accessing patient files
- **Employee dishonesty,** e.g., disclosing health records
- **Improper disposal,** e.g., the hard drive in the office printer
- **Third-party disclosure,** e.g., business associates or subcontractors who ineffectively protect protected health information (PHI)
- **Unauthorized discussion of medical conditions,** e.g., while in a waiting room
- **Sharing incorrect medical information,** e.g., you receive a treatment plan via email that isn't yours
- **Emailing or texting patient information,** e.g., receptionist emails patient information
- **Posting on social media,** e.g., picture of a patient's disease or treatment, even without the patient's name, is posted on social media
- **Lack of prior authorization information for release,** e.g., disclosure of any individual's PHI that's not used for treatment, payment, or healthcare operations or that falls under the Privacy rule.

Does an editable blockchain offer advantages to healthcare entities that are part of the health delivery system? To address this question, let's split this into two separate questions: (1) value of blockchains and (2) benefits of editable blockchains.

Blockchain technology, when applied to healthcare, can absolutely improve the trust between doctors and patients. To answer the second part of this question, we asked Bernardo Magri, author and researcher, for his thoughts. For Magri, the benefits of blockchains in healthcare settings are quite evident. Magri then addressed the potential benefits. The chameleon key is only given to the healthcare privacy officer.

However, we do not expect a privacy officer to run the entire blockchain or produce transactions about payments or add health records. The privacy officer would be called in when records must be expunged because of HIPAA or another regulation violation. The role of the healthcare privacy officer is expanding. As data, information, and intelligent analytics become a foundational element of every healthcare organization, the protection of health information is a critical growth and sustainability strategy.

IN PRACTICE

The paper, "Redactable Blockchain or Rewriting History in Bitcoin and Friends," elaborates on a proof-of-concept implementation to redact a Bitcoin application using three distinct functions: GenerateKey (create the "trapdoor key"), ChameleonHash (computes hash—from the message and random number), and HashCollision (outputs new random number for reference later). This scenario was then modeled using a regression test network feature of the Bitcoin core network.

This framework opens the ability to redact and compress the content of blocks in virtually any blockchain-based technology. Are editable blockchains merely a form of modern censorship, disguised as flexibility for all but the chosen few? Time will tell.

It's evident that industries are very curious about editable blockchains. Editable blockchains have officially entered the Innovation Trigger stage of the Hype Cycle.

MIT Dives Into Blockchain

Not all researchers are interested in editable blockchains. Bitcoin, Ethereum, and Hyperledger offer different approaches and various technology stacks to capture the emerging capabilities of the blockchain.

The World Wide Web Consortium (W3C) presented the "Blockchains and the Web: A W3C Workshop on Distributed

Ledgers on the Web" workshop, hosted by the MIT Media Lab. Exploring the identity, value exchange, asset recording, consortium frameworks, and reputation systems all fall within the mystique of the blockchain technologies. Blockchain platforms could offer distributed micro-services that can be applied to the web, enabling personalization of services using smart contracts.

What form will the next pseudonymous low-level messaging system or incentivization framework take? Innovators converged at the MIT Media Lab to get answers—by consensus.

MIT'S W3C WORKSHOP ON THE WEB

The allure and possibilities surrounding blockchain have increased over the last several years but erupted over the last six months. The MIT Media Lab workshop called, "Blockchains and the Web: A W3C Workshop on Distributed Ledgers on the Web," was held at the MIT Media Lab in Cambridge, Massachusetts, USA. Goals of the workshop included:

- Core technical components of blockchains and their overlap with the Web, such as:
  - Blockchain APIs such as JavaScript or REST APIs
  - Blockchain primitives such as transaction initiation, key signing, and wallet management
  - Ledger interchange formats and protocols
  - Smart contracts and conditional execution contexts
- Application areas, such as:
  - Identity systems including privacy, security, and confidentiality factors
  - Rights expression and licensing
  - Decentralized processing, computing, and storage infrastructure
- Other considerations such as:
  - Optimal use cases for blockchains

- ○ Surveys of existing blockchain software systems
- ○ Testing mechanisms to increase interoperability, robustness, stability, and confidence in blockchain systems

The particular focus was on representatives from the Bitcoin community: communities such as Hyperledger and Ethereum; browser developers interested in adding support for blockchain APIs, identity systems, digital currency projects, security, privacy researchers, and financial institutions; and developers of blockchain systems who want to improve interoperability. The objective of the W3C workshop was to identify areas that need web standardization and incubation to ensure the right steps are taken for the key stakeholders involved.

The MIT Media Lab, in early June 2016, started collecting position statements (name, background, links to resources, and topics of interest focusing on the what, not the how) and expression-of-interest statements (name, organization, bio, goals, and workshop goals) for potential participants interested in attending the workshop.[15][16] The goals and objectives varied widely, and it was great to see a wide range of uses for blockchain.

BLOCKCHAIN TOPICS OF INTEREST

The W3C program committee was jointly co-chaired by Doug Schepers, W3C; Daniel Buchner, Blockchain Identity Program Manager, Microsoft; Neha Narula, Director of Digital Currency Initiative (DCI), MIT; and Dazza Greenwood, MIT Media Lab.

The "W3C Blockchain and the Web" committee's diversity is expansive and includes members from Blockstream, IPFS, LedgerX, Intel, Microsoft, Eris Industries, NTT, IBM Blockchain Labs, MIT Media Lab, W3C, ConsenSys, PayGate, BSafe.network, CELLOS consortium, BigchainDB, MIT Digital Currency Initiative (DCI), Blockstack, EthCore, Monegraph, String, Dfinity, and Ethereum.

nts who requested to join the workshop were
k their interest across ten topics, and, after 53
Below is that ranking:

- Blockchain APIs, such as JavaScript or REST APIs
- Blockchain primitives such as transaction initiation, key signing, and wallet management
- Ledger interchange formats and protocols
- Smart contracts and conditional execution contexts
- Identity systems, including privacy, security, and confidentiality factors
- Rights expression and licensing
- Decentralized processing, computing, and storage infrastructure
- Optimal use cases for blockchains
- Surveys of existing blockchain software systems
- Testing mechanisms to increase interoperability, robustness, stability, and confidence in blockchain systems

A noteworthy addition to the "Blockchains and the Web: A W3C Workshop on Distributed Ledgers on the Web" workshop speaking line-up was Arvind Narayanan, an assistant professor of computer science at Princeton. His focus centers around information privacy and security. His blogs, *Freedom to Tinker* and *33 Bits of Entropy*, have insightful pieces of information that can have you lost in wonder for hours.[17][18]

Narayanan's course, titled, "Bitcoin and Cryptocurrency Technologies," from Princeton University, is available through Coursera.[19] The course is quite popular, with over 35,000 students attending the latest class offered, which introduced students to crypto and computer science.

The core course topics include: intro to crypto and cryptocurrencies; how Bitcoin achieves decentralization; mechanics of Bitcoin; how to store and use Bitcoins; Bitcoin mining, Bitcoin and anonymity, community, politics, and regulation; alternative mining puzzles; Bitcoin as a platform; altcoins and the cryptocurrency ecosystem; the future of Bitcoin; and the history of cryptocurrencies.

Interested readers can opt-in for notification when the course is open. Narayanan also offers a detailed (308-page) downloadable textbook, *Bitcoin and Crytocurrency Technology*, is publicly accessible for free and available now from Princeton University Press.[20] The book does a thorough job of explaining underlying views regarding what Bitcoin is and how it works.

His course addresses the following important questions about Bitcoin:

- How does Bitcoin work?
- What makes it different?
- How secure are your bitcoins?
- How anonymous are Bitcoin users?
- What applications can we build using Bitcoin as a platform?
- Can cryptocurrencies be regulated?
- If we were designing a new cryptocurrency today, what would we change?
- What might the future hold?

MIT BLOCKCHAIN WORKSHOP HANGOUTS SERIES

How does identity-related information get safely published to a public ledger without violating an individual's privacy? Are verifiable claims and their standardizations the future? The W3C workshop undoubtedly uncovered even more blockchain possibilities.

First responders and emergency workers could be authenticated to gain protected site access or cross-jurisdiction interoperability, utilization of centralized key management (biometric sensors, native security features, integration with web applications, including key recovery), or connected device self-authentication.

During the workshop, interest quickly turned to healthcare and the potential to drive change with healthcare interoperability, an interaction that affects every human being.

The Potential for Blockchain

CIOs want to be innovative and have aspirations to be leaders among leaders. In the quest to achieve this, understanding where innovators go for innovation is important.

Do you have technology teams already involved in the W3C? You should. Is your organization participating in a company or university innovation lab? It should. Through collaboration, innovation grows.

The W3C blockchain interoperability workshop at MIT is an incubator for inspiration and a source for new perspectives. The workshop might have even provided some answers. But we all know that asking questions is more fun.

As you read the workshops highlights below, ask yourself, in your role as a leader, these three questions:

- Is my company an innovation leader?
- How should my organization get involved in setting standards?
- Who in my organization should get involved?

If you're not leading, you're lagging—and chasing innovation rarely works!

MAGICAL COLLABORATION

The first day of the workshop started with an introduction by Doug Schepers of World Wide Web Consortium. He framed the two-day workshop around a vision of enabling collaboration and engaging in technical discussions. The two days were organized primarily around lightning talks—five-minute topic introductions to spark conversations. Four subject areas created the framework for the workshops:

1. **Identity:** reputation, personal data BYC, various aspects of identity
2. **Provenance:** licensing of IP, assets, and services
3. **Blockchain primitives and APIs:** browser-like features, consensus protocols, standard data formats
4. **Kitchen sink:** everything else that didn't fit the above

Schepers asked each table to come up with one primary theme that represented a magical and powerful collaboration story. The underlying goal was to identify the pieces of successful collaborations. Below is an abridged version of the big hitters.

1. Collaborative consensus is the secret sauce.
2. Everyone agreed that friction can be productive.
3. The shared problem statement is an evolving document.
4. Recognize when you're finished and when to stop.
5. You want motivation that might not be rational.
6. Flexibility and diversity are important.
7. Fail fast by staying focused.
8. Break down information and take ownership of issues.
9. Shed concerns about ecosystem ownership.
10. Encourage early adopters with hands-on play.

W3C STANDARDS WORKGROUPS

Wendy Selzer, with W3C, kicked off the day with "Intro to W3C standards," a presentation that also provided an excellent outline of the W3C organization.

The World Wide Web Consortium is an international community where member organizations, a full-time staff, and the public work together to develop Web standards. The mission of W3C is to lead the Web to its full potential with over 400 member organizations participating in shaping the future of standards. Selzer discussed several workgroups that were making strong progress toward standards in the Web space. Currently, W3C has over 40 active workgroups.

If your organization doesn't yet have technical leaders involved in these groups, know that it's advantageous to be engaged in creating the standards versus blindly having to adhere to them.

1. **Web authorization (GitHub):** to define a client-side API providing strong authentication functionality to Web Applications.

2. **Web cryptography:** to define a high-level API providing standard cryptographic functionality to Web Applications.

3. **Web application security:** to define a high-level API providing standard cryptographic functionality to Web Applications.

4. **Web payments:** to make payments easier and more secure on the Web.

5. **Privacy (Interest Group):** to improve the support of privacy in Web standards by monitoring ongoing privacy issues that affect the Web.

6. **Web platform:** to continue the development of the HTML language, providing specifications that enable improved client-side application development on the Web (including APIs).

7. **Web performance:** to provide methods to observe and improve aspects of application performance of user agent features and APIs.

8. **Cascading Style Sheets (CSS):** to develop and maintain CSS.

9. **HTML media extensions:** to continue the development of the HTML language as well as the development of APIs for interacting with in-memory representations of resources that use the HTML language.

10. **Web real-time communications:** to define client-side APIs to enable Real-Time Communications in Web browsers.

11. **Verifiable claims task force:** to determine if a W3C
    Working Group should be created to standardize
    technology around a verifiable claims ecosystem (cre-
    dentials, attestations).
12. **Private key JavaScript (PKLjs):** pre-standards phase.

Blockchain Practical Examples

Arvind Narayanan followed with a priming presentation. Not
a typical presentation, which we all hate, but more like a discussion igniter.

Narayanan began by asking: How do we marry the power
of the blockchain with the reach of the Web? There were a
lot of great examples over the course of the workshop. I'll
highlight three of the best thought provokers.

1. **A USB-based car key for car sharing:** in general,
   signatures would be uploaded to the blockchain.
   Then, using Bluetooth, the car would query the key,
   requesting proofs, resulting in the temporary authorization enabling the individual to drive the vehicle.
   This entire transaction would be verifiable by the car,
   including using proof-of-work.
2. **Blockchain receipts for your hamburger:** We've all
   purchased a hamburger, but what if you could have
   your hamburger stamped with a unique hash to show
   the audit trail (proof the location was inspected, not
   necessarily who made the burger; this is similar to
   chain-of-custody or provenance). What if every food
   receipt in the world became proof?
3. **Graceful failure:** Between 1845 and 1957, bridges fell
   with frightening frequency. Today, we know when
   they're going to fail; we just don't fix them. Adding
   traffic lights to bridges, linked to the blockchain, could
   prevent cars from passing when a suspension wire
   sensor fails. Let's redefine the term "graceful failure."

ARCHIVAL BOND

The archival bond is a concept in archival theory referring to the relationship that each archival record has with other records produced as part of the same transaction and located within the same grouping.

This concept is primarily associated with Luciana Duranti, a professor of archival science at the School of Library, Archival, and Information Studies at the University of British Columbia, Canada, who first proposed the concept with Heather MacNeil. MacNeil conducted research into the integrity of electronic records and the results were published in her 1996 paper, "The Protection of the Integrity of Electronic Records."[21]

When we apply this concept, records won't be on the blockchain but, rather, only the hashes would reside on the blockchain (or related links or mappings). Does this mean library science and archival studies will be rising educational majors? Will the "Chief Archival Officer" be the newest wave to enter the c-suite?

When Change is Unexpected

Self-sovereignty and identity anonymity hold the code to unlock the potential for blockchain to change patient health. The architecture of the Internet has changed forever.

Technological change forces economic growth. Technology extends the science of discovery and produces artifacts used in everyday life. It's the small technical discoveries that make larger scientific endeavors possible. It's also these seemingly unrelated breakthroughs that make their way into our daily lives.

APPARENTLY INSIGNIFICANT DISCOVERIES BECOME SIGNIFICANT

In the 1960s, NASA conducted an extensive test program to investigate the effects of pavement texture on wet runways. The goal was to better understand braking performance and reduce the incidence of aircraft hydroplaning. The result of years of technical and scientific studies was that, in 1967, grooving of pavement became an accepted technique for improving the safety of commercial runways.

One of the first runways to feature safety grooving was the Kennedy Space Center's landing strip. However, the applications of this technique extended well beyond NASA facilities. According to the Space Foundation, safety grooving was later included on such potentially hazardous surfaces as interstate highway curves and overpasses; pedestrian walkways, ramps, and steps; playgrounds; railroad station platforms; swimming pool decks; cattle holding pens; and slick working areas in industrial sites such as refineries, meat-packing plants, and food processing facilities.

If you asked a cattle rancher in 1970 if his work would be affected by NASA's research on braking patterns exploring ground vertical load and the instantaneous tire-ground friction coefficient or free-rolling wheel angular velocity, the answer would probably have been an emphatic "not a chance." Likewise, if you'd told the workers on a road crew in 1970 that they'd be spending many years of their lives adding grooves to the surfaces of existing highways, bridges, and exit ramps, their response would have been less than welcoming. It would have been impossible to convince these professionals of the coming changes.

The impact of technology on daily life starts with scientific and technological discoveries that initially appear isolated or narrow in context. But we know better.

5 MIT Projects to Watch

The MIT Internet Trust Consortium, established in 2007, focuses on developing interoperable technologies around identity, trust, and data. The consortium's mission is to develop open-source components for the Internet's emerging personal data ecosystem in which people, organizations, and computers can manage access to their data more efficiently and equitably. The goal is to build emerging personal data ecosystems for individuals and organizations. That ideological desire fits in nicely with the growth of blockchain technologies.

Currently, there are five cutting-edge MIT projects that could change the future of the Internet using blockchain technologies: MIT ChainAnchor, (permissioned blockchains); Project Enigma (autonomous control of personal data); OpenPDS2.0 (a personal metadata management framework); DataHub (a platform with the ability to collaboratively analyze data); and Distributed User Managed Access Systems (DUMAS—a protocol for authorizing and accessing online personal data).

The white papers for each project are interesting to read. When reading with a healthcare mindset, it's easy to explore how functionality could extend into the health and wellness industries.

MIT CHAINANCHOR

The proposed permissioned blockchain system is in contrast to the permissionless and public blockchains in Bitcoin. The system addresses identity and access control within shared, permissioned blockchains, providing anonymous but verifiable identities for entities on the blockchain.

As an example of applying ChainAnchor to healthcare, participants of a medical study could maintain their privacy through the use of a verifiable anonymous identity when contributing (executing transactions on the blockchains).

PROJECT ENIGMA

Enigma is a peer-to-peer network that allows users to share their data with cryptographic privacy guarantees. The decentralized computational platform enables "privacy by design." The white paper says that, for example, "a group of people can provide access to their salary, and together compute the average wage of the group. Each participant learns their relative position in the group, but learns nothing about other members' salaries."[22] Sharing information today is irreversible; once shared, a user is unable to take that data back. With Enigma, data access is reversible and controllable. Only the original data owners have access to raw data.

In the context of healthcare, patients could share information regarding personal genomics linked to disease registries and clinical treatments aligned to healthcare outcomes, knowing that their original data wasn't shared.

OPENPDS2.0

OpenPDS introduces SafeAnswers, an innovative way to protect metadata (application, document, file, or embedded) at an individual level.

SafeAnswers "allows services to ask questions whose answers are calculated against the metadata instead of trying to anonymize individuals' metadata."[23] SafeAnswers gives individuals the ability to share their personal metadata safely through a question-and-answer system.

Previous mechanisms for storing personal metadata (cloud storage systems and personal data repositories) don't offer data aggregation mechanisms. The challenge in data protection continues to be that once access is enabled, the data is broadly accessible. SafeAnswers reduces the dimensionality of the metadata before it leaves the safe environment, therefore reducing the threat profile and helping to ensure data privacy.

Healthcare metadata examples could include patient account number, the patient's first and last name, and date of admission. Healthcare research could benefit from using aggregated metadata from patients without sharing the raw data. Research entities would send questions to an individual's personal data store (PDS). This PDS would respond with an answer.

Today, if metadata information were provided to researchers or accessed from a phone application, the patient could disable (uninstall) the app but wouldn't know what information was shared.

With the SafeAnswers system, a patient potentially would use their PDS URL to provide access to the health app. All of the patient's metadata, therefore, could be tracked and recorded—visible to the patient. Later, the patient could access the metadata that the application was using to create inferences.

Also, the patient could permanently remove the metadata that the application was consuming by either limiting or permanently restricting future access. No trusted third party. No entity to monitor access. Data shared anonymously.

DISCOVERIES THAT TRANSFORM SOCIETY

The DataHub project and the Distributed User Managed Access Systems (DUMAS) projects offer additional pieces to solve the challenge of exchanging information while maintaining identity anonymity. Maybe they can apply to healthcare—if we're creative.

Highly technical advances have shaped the social economy for centuries. The creation of the sickle, a handheld agricultural tool with a curved blade typically used for harvesting grain crops, had a profound impact on the Neolithic Revolution (Agricultural Revolution). Who would have imagined when it was invented (18000 to 8000 B.C.) that the sickle would form the basis for modern kitchen knives with serrated edges?

Small, seemingly insignificant discoveries transform societies. How blockchain technologies will affect people on a daily basis is waiting to be discovered. When blockchain applications enhance our lives, they may become as commonplace as highway grooves.

"All progress is precarious, and the solution of one problem brings us face to face with another problem."

— MARTIN LUTHER KING, JR.

CHAPTER 3

IBM BLOCKCHAIN SOLUTIONS

The potential for blockchain technology is limited only by our imaginations. The IBM Blockchain service on Bluemix helps you save time writing applications in chaincode.

Let's unwrap IBM's offering and explore how your technology team will benefit from this advancement. Think back. Remember the time you played with your first LEGO kit? It wasn't just a stationary plastic toy, used for construction. These bricks lived and breathed—they came to life.

Anything can be created with LEGO—from people that talk to mythical creatures and even entire villages that launch spaceships. The possibilities are only limited by your imagination. Consider the world you could build if it was limited only by your creativity. That's the world where we all should live.

What if we didn't know we could only build a house or a car out of LEGO? What if there was no limit to the possibilities? This is the challenge we have with blockchain. Blockchain technologies are much like that first LEGO set you received as a child. We don't have to force blockchain to transform into our existing models; blockchain technologies can enable new models. What if tomorrow's growth from blockchain isn't linear? This is how great minds think. They use first-principle thinking: Original ideas aren't born from past assumptions; they emerge from the strategic and calculated alignment of ideas into unpredictable, unusual combinations, creating new causes.

The Limitless Wonder of LEGOs

Denmark carpenter Ole Kirk Christiansen created the wooden toy blocks that eventually became LEGOs in his garage in 1932. In 1934, Christiansen founded a company called the LEGO Group, a name derived from the Danish phrase leg godt, which means "play well."

In 1950, the plastic bricks were launched, quickly followed by the biplane and motorized truck set in the 1960s. In the 1970s, LEGO Ville was introduced, allowing children to create entire villages to explore. Fire engines, moon landings, the first 12-volt motor train series, and even LEGOLand ships were introduced and quickly adopted globally across 42 countries. Christiansen grew the company from one person to almost 6,000 by 1987. Today, LEGO products are sold in more than 140 countries.

Why did it take nearly 50 years to introduce the idea of a LEGO Village? From the first LEGO Numskull Jack on the Goat to the 2016 Volkswagen Beetle kit, innovation is about bringing the impossible to life. Innovation isn't linear.

IBM's Blockchain Offering

Recently, IBM launched Blockchain Cloud Services on Linux-ONE, a high-security business network.[1] The primary driver behind the release was to give customers solutions to address the privacy and interoperability challenges of blockchain ecosystems.

IBM LinuxOne is open source and was designed for the app economy. Today, IBM LinuxOne is the most efficient, robust, and secure Linux platform available.[2] Why is it more efficient?

IBM LinuxOne has 2x the performance for MongoDB, MariaDB, and PostgreSQL plus 30 billion RESTful (architectural style of interactions between data elements rather than implementation details) web interactions a day on Node.js and MongoDB, supported by 1.5 more containers and 4x faster analytics on Docker (a platform to build and ship distributed apps).

Two Environments Support the IBM Blockchain

There are two versions (environments) that are capable of running the IBM Blockchain on IBM Bluemix: (1) the Starter Developer and (2) the High-Security Business Network.

The Starter Developer runs on the SoftLayer platform, which supports a shared multitenant environment to develop and test levels of security performance and availability. The platform includes the testing consensus and availability Practical Byzantine Fault Tolerance (PBFT) consensus protocol.[3]

The PBFT consensus protocol maintains the order of transactions on the blockchain network and helps to avoid threats to this decree. This environment doesn't include a Secure Services Container (SSC)—a secure environment with advanced cryptography and security—but it does include a dashboard monitor.

The High-Security Business Network (HSBN) runs on IBM LinuxONE and is only available on an isolated, single-tenant environment. It simulates enterprise network and test levels of security, performance, and availability. The HSBN includes the SSC, which is deployed as an appliance that provides the base infrastructure for hosting blockchain services.

According to IBM, the appliance combines operating systems, Docker, middleware, and software components that work autonomously and provide core services and infrastructure with optimized security. The PBFT consensus protocol is leveraged in this environment, and HSBN includes a dashboard monitor. It's worth noting that the High-Security Business Network is in beta only, and IBM's approval is required to access this environment.

Start My Blockchain Network

If you're interested in setting up a development environment with validating nodes and a security service, there are three main steps involved in providing your team with a proof-of-concept environment.

1. **Create service:** Log-in to the landing page for the Blockchain DevOps Service and add a service (service name and credential name, and then a development environment plan).[4]

2. **Monitor network:** Once on the service dashboard, you're able to manage the network and launch the blockchain monitor for the blockchain network you just created.

3. **Install chaincode examples:** With this dashboard, you'll be able to access discovery and API routes for the peers on your network, view chaincode containers, see real-time logs and troubleshoot chaincode that fails to execute, and deploy one of several available chaincode examples.

There are four tutorials and chaincode samples of IBM Blockchain on GitHub; your team can immediately upload the following into your newly created environment:

1. IBM Marbles Demo[5]
2. IBM Commercial Paper Demo[6]
3. IBM Car Lease Demo[7]
4. Art Auction Demo.[8]

BENEFITS OF IBM BLOCKCHAIN

There are several ways to set up and get your team started exploring the wonders of blockchain technologies. It's exciting to consider new revenue streams as we integrate blockchain technologies into our existing business ecosystems. However, we do need to balance the inherent risk of introducing new technologies.

Use your imagination to discover new ways to improve your customer interactions utilizing blockchain technologies.

And remember, "If you cry from both eyes, you probably stepped on a LEGO." Innovation is a process. Even experts can step on LEGOs, but they step on them less often.

IBM's Global Solutions

IBM is creating solutions to connect the global healthcare delivery system. A recent IBM Institute for Business Value survey found the trailblazers of blockchain adoption will focus on three areas: clinical trial records, regulatory compliance, and medical/health records.

Which industry is the most progressive? Healthcare won't appear on most lists, but a recent study by the IBM Institute for Business Value revealed that, surprisingly, healthcare executives are setting the pace of blockchain adoption.[9]

The survey, conducted for IBM by The Economist Intelligence Unit, found that 16 percent of healthcare executives expect to implement commercial blockchain solutions at scale by the end of 2017.

Integrating artificial intelligence with machine learning, experimenting with virtual reality, and robotic process automation are several of the ways that healthcare executives are capturing the benefits for patients while skillfully dodging regulatory compliance obstacles.

The business of disruption isn't where you'd expect it to be—at patient experience. Patient interactions, while marginally improving, aren't dramatically transforming. There are pools of revolution here or there, but largely trends firmly grip the status quo. The major shift of transformative innovation is happening with the introduction of new business models, and blockchain is positioned to lead this charge.

INNOVATIVE INSIGHTS

IBM brought together an impressive group of leaders to design and execute its study, which surveyed 200 healthcare executives across 16 countries—from payers to providers. IBM employees who were part of this design team included Sean Hogan, global industry general manager for healthcare and life sciences; Heather Fraser, global healthcare and life sciences leader; Peter Korsten, vice president of global thought leadership and eminence; Venna Pureswaran, blockchain research leader; and Ramesh Gopinath, vice president for blockchain solutions and research.

The core IBM team was reinforced by dozens more amazing industry contributors. Together, the team produced an insightful analysis of the complex world of blockchain technologies and defined the new vectors for growth and disruption.

IBM presented a view contrary to survey results, which indicated that executives are expecting healthcare to set the pace of innovation slightly ahead of the financial services industry—with little disruption. The IBM Institute for Business Value survey expanded upon four questions:

1. What's the cadence and pace of healthcare trailblazers?
2. How would new benefits and business models significantly reduce the time, cost, and risks associated with how they operate?
3. Where would the new vectors for growth and disruption occur, shifting profit pools?
4. How fast should executives adopt blockchain for their organizations?

TRAILBLAZERS OF ADOPTION

Are healthcare executives complacent and comfortable with how patient care is delivered? It's possible. However, there may be another answer. Healthcare executives predicted transformational innovation to occur for blockchain in 2017.

The IBM Institute for Business Value blockchain survey identified nine areas where transformation and disruption are likely to emerge:

1. Medical device data integration (cited as an area of "some disruption" by 65 percent of respondents)
2. Asset management (60 percent)
3. Medical and health records (42 percent)
4. Clinical trial records (40 percent)
5. Adverse event safety monitoring (39 percent)
6. Medication and treatment adherence (36 percent)
7. Regulatory compliance (34 percent)
8. Billing and claims management (33 percent)
9. Contract management (32 percent)

The survey results indicate that disruption rarely emerges from a single process. Transformational innovation forms when organizations voluntarily or involuntarily reconsider organizational boundaries. North American respondents lagged other regions in innovation, with only 8 percent identifying their organizations as trailblazers. The initial first-mover advantages to adopting blockchain technology appear weak. The value of early collaborations and new partnerships has yet to be defined.

REDUCING FRICTIONS

The IBM Institute for Business Value blockchain survey called out nine frictions that blockchain is expected to significantly impact:

1. Imperfect information
2. Inaccessible information
3. Informational risks
4. Transaction costs
5. Degrees of separation
6. Inaccessible marketplaces
7. Restrictive regulations

8. Institutional inertia
9. Invisible threats

A reduction of misinformation that improves interactions and accelerates healthcare delivery by reducing intermediaries has proved to be the most impactful.

As boundaries between payers and providers become less visible, it's apparent that data verification and cost-delay frictions impact trust. How will organizations respond to blockchain opportunities? Executives are answering with additional investments in blockchain technologies.

ESTABLISHING 'TRUTH, NOT TRUST' WITH NEW BUSINESS MODELS

The private sector of healthcare requires patients to trust. Trust that their medical information is protected. Trust that treatment is appropriate to the symptoms. Trust that the care they receive is tailored to their needs.

The value of blockchain isn't about the technology. Blockchain's value is harnessed in the transformative effect of new business models—business models based on "truth, not trust."

Blockchain provides proof. Proof that patient medical information is protected. Proof that patient treatment is appropriate. Proof that patient care is personalized.

Across the board, the survey results indicate executives will make the following investments by 2018:

1. Medical and health records (94 percent)
2. Billing and claims management (94 percent)
3. Medical devices and data integration (92 percent)
4. Asset management (91 percent)
5. Contract management (90 percent)
6. Medication and treatment adherence (89 percent)
7. Clinical trial records (88 percent)
8. Regulatory compliance (87 percent)
9. Adverse event safety monitoring (86 percent)

A BLOCK-BY-BLOCK APPROACH TO BETTER CARE

The IBM Institute for Business Value report gives executives a foundation to be curious. Executives are encouraged to ask questions and inquire about how these components work together to produce value. The healthcare trailblazers are empowering patients to take ownership of their data, as trusted peer-to-peer care networks compete for on-demand services.

Medical health records silos, medical device data vaporware, and limited outcomes for adverse events are moving toward a new business model. The IBM report is loaded with additional information for executives. Here are three findings to keep you asking questions:

- Nine in 10 healthcare organizations by 2018 plan to finance blockchain applications initiatives.
- As mentioned earlier, 16 percent of healthcare trailblazers expect to have a commercial solution at scale by 2017.
- Six in 10 healthcare trailblazers anticipate blockchains will help them access new markets and keep trusted information secure.

The IBM report prepares executives to ask the right questions—keeping patients at the center.

An Evolution of Potential

Standardization is holding blockchain back. From IP to ARPANET, let's explore the fabric needed for blockchain's adoption in healthcare.

Blockchain is part of the Internet-of-Things, the Fifth Wave of the Internet. In 1961, Leonard Kleinrock, a professor of computer science at UCLA, wrote about ARPANET and developed the first theory of packet switching.[10] The first node of the Internet was born in September 1969. The days of 1969 seem like eons ago, but tearing a page from the history of the Internet may help us forecast tomorrow's blockchain trends. A foundational blockchain fabric must be established before blockchain will become mainstream and accessible to the company down the street.

BLOOMING OF BLOCKCHAIN APPLICATIONS

Healthcare-related blockchain applications are sprouting up all around us. The Gem platform uses multi-signature, hardware security modules (HSMs) and cryptographic keychains to address identity and information-access security, which acts as an application-layer blockchain protocol. Factom is looking to secure data and possibly medical records using the technology behind bitcoin. Guardtime, a cyber-security provider that uses blockchain systems to ensure the integrity of data, is partnering with the Estonian e-Health Authority to secure over a million healthcare records. MedVault is a proof-of-concept that will allow patients to record medical information on the Bitcoin blockchain. MedVault works with Colu for digital assets issuance and management on top of the bitcoin blockchain using API and SDKs.

Companies around the globe are exploring the value of blockchain. Will every business have to build a full blockchain stack from scratch? Ethereum and others have built an entire blockchain stack, including the application layer, hoping to corner the market. R3 (R3CEV LLC) isn't building a blockchain. R3 Corda is focusing on individual agreements between firms ("state objects," governed by "contract code" and associated "legal prose"). The Hyperledger project is building the fabric of the blockchain.

HYPERLEDGER AND THE LINUX FOUNDATION

The Hyperledger project is led but not owned by IBM and overseen by the Linux Foundation. The project's objective is to create a framework to allow the ability to transfer assets digitally. The HyperLedger project is a collaboration of some of the most innovative companies to create an operating system for interactions and has the potential to vastly reduce the cost and complexity of getting things done.

The best and brightest companies across finance, banking, Internet of Things, supply chains, manufacturing, and technology are joining the cause. As of April 2016, 40 companies were committed to this mission. The companies involved in the collaboration include: Accenture, CME Group, Deutsche Borse Group, Digital Asset, DTCC, Fujitsu, Hitachi, IBM, Intel, J.P.Morgan, R3, ABN-AMRO, ANZ, Blockchain, Blockstream, bloq, BNY Mellon, Casastone, CISCO, CLS, Consensys, CREDITS, Evue Digital Labs, Gem, guardtime, intellect, itBit, Milligan Partners, Montran, NEC, NTT DATA, Red Hat, Ribbit.me, State Street, Swift, symbiont, tequa creek, Thomson Reuters, vmware, and Wells Fargo. Other companies are rapidly coming on board.

BLOCKCHAIN'S OPEN SOURCE FABRIC

Similar to standard network protocols, a foundational layer must be in place for other systems to operate and build. This lack of foundation would be akin to every company rewriting Linux or Windows to deploy its applications. These core layers must be established before blockchain applications can be built. We can't build on Layer 7 of the Open System Interconnect model without the benefit of supporting layer stability. Consortiums are forming to do just that.

The Hyperledger project is already on GitHub. Ripple has contributed with an open-source, C++ implementation of a public and distributed ledger. IBM added an Open Blockchain (OBC) that's a low-level blockchain fabric designed to meet the requirements of a variety of industry-focused use cases.[11] According to GitHub, "the central elements of this implementation are smart contracts (what IBM calls chaincode, the embedded business logic that enables the definition of assets and provides the ability to write transaction instructions), digital assets, record repositories, a decentralized network providing consensus, and cryptographic security."[12]

Digital Asset Holdings contributed an enterprise-ready blockchain server with a client API; this adds an append-only log of financial transactions designed to be replicated at multiple organizations without centralized control.[13] Blockstream contributed the Elements Project, a modularized fork of the Bitcoin codebase that adds several significant improvements called "Elements." Elements is an open-source, protocol-level technology. Developers can use Elements to extend the functionality of Bitcoin and explore new applications of the blockchain.[14]

GitHub is the open-source repository that Hyperledger uses for collaboration. IBM's Bluemix offers chaincode. Open-source collaborators will construct the future fabric of the blockchain.

Blockchain is growing faster today than the Internet during the initial excitement in 1995. Open-source fabrics will provide the foundation for innovation as companies collaborate to build the Internet's Fifth Wave.

"Every problem has in it the seeds of its own solution. If you don't have any problems, you don't get any seeds."

— NORMAN VINCENT

CHAPTER 4

MICROSOFT'S BLOCKCHAIN SOLUTION

Identity, security, and cryptography baked into middleware. Customized performance for blockchains. Technology teams just got more productive.

Marley Gray, director of BizDev & Strategy (including blockchain business development), Cloud, and Enterprise at Microsoft, posted an update to GitHub providing an overview of Bletchley.

The white paper was published six days after Microsoft's announcement of Project Bletchley and goes on to say that Project Bletchley is a set of tools for supporting SmartContracts on the blockchain, enabling secure access to off-chain information.[1] The project supports open standards for protocol-level implementations of peer-to-peer networking, consensus, database, and virtual machines, which are vital to establishing trust within a blockchain ecosystem.

Bletchley is a middleware tool set for developers and provides an ecosystem to enable implementing identity, security, cryptography, scale, tooling, management, monitoring, and reporting both on and off the blockchain.

Client-Driven Performance Flexibility

What Bletchley offers is performance flexibility for core, kernel, and universal protocols. For example, a banking application will have different requirements for transactional, processing, and nonfunctional requirements for scale than would a nonprofit using a basic digital ledger to record donations.

The two-tier client-server architectures are multitier, computing architectures in which an entire application is distributed as two distinct layers or tiers. In this case, the presentation layer and data layer run on the server. In contrast, three-tier or n-tier architecture is usually separated into three major sections: The presentation/front-end tier, the business/application tier, and the data/back-end tier.

The process of blockchain architectures experienced a similar evolution as tier-level client architectures. Blockchain 1.0—a simple state machine—used logic (stored procedures) to record transactions in sequence, where referential integrity was implemented through the use of primary keys (PK) and foreign keys (FK). Blockchain 2.0—state machine and code—added SmartContracts. The 2.0 version also leverages PK and FK; however, Blockchain 2.0 also contains logic (code like a stored procedure) that can be executed. Blockchain 3.0—state machine and code and cryptlets—allows for improved interoperability and scale on and off the blockchain.

As a general clarification, there are some additional differences regarding tokenization and instantiation of transactions that are beyond the scope of this book.

Microsoft also introduces the idea of the enterprise consortium node. In these scenarios, the client system makes a request, and the request is given to a future node (block database, state, history) that's connected to the block database (state and history, signing, VM, and consensus).

In short, the modular framework can choose the best components to fulfill the client request. We're starting to reach the ability to handle dynamic, scalable requests.

Getting Off-Chain Data

Cryptlets establish the foundation for Microsoft's security blockchain middleware, run as a cloud-based service, and are provider-agnostic. Previously, when making data requests outside a SmartContract, the authenticity was broken for dependent transactions. For example: If you're running an app on your phone and you need to process an order, you need your payment information stored in another SmartContract. Another example would be: While running a phone app, you make a request to view your medical information, but when you click on your lab results details, a call (to the lab's Smart-Contract) is required to access that information (outside of the existing SmartContract). Today, the effect is that the pure integrity of the transaction is broken.

Cryptlets live off the blockchain and execute within a secure, trusted container and communicate using secure channels. Cryptlets can also be written in any programming language and are called or instantiated by a CryptoDelegate (with the SmartContract). Cryptlets come in two flavors: Utility and Contract. Utility provides core infrastructure and middleware services, e.g., encryption, time and date events, external data access, and authentication services. Contract provides all the execution logic and securely stores the data in the SmartContract. Contract Cryptlets don't run on the blockchain and therefore can execute in parallel on vertically scaled systems.

Blockchain Middleware

The idea of "winner takes all" doesn't apply to blockchains. The number of players on the field is exploding, and consortiums are required to play to win. Microsoft gets that multiple players are required for effective blockchain outcomes and to fuel deeper rapid application development. As a result, Microsoft has touted blockchain middleware as the "Enterprise Consortium Distributed Ledger Fabric" evolving into APIs and platform-as-a-service. Is this the real fix for interoperability for payments, health, property, and provenance? It might not fix everything, but it's a strong start to solving a huge problem.

The Microsoft blockchain middleware layer provides these core services as explained in the white paper:[2]

1. **Identity and Certificate Services:** authentication, authorization, key issuance, storage, Cryptlet registration, access, and life-cycle management.
2. **Encryption Services:** partial payload encryption.
3. **Cryptlet Services:** attested hosting for cryptlets to be securely invoked by CryptoDelegates in SmartContracts.
4. **Blockchain Gateway Services:** Interledger-like services to allow for SmartContracts and tokenized objects to be passed among different ledger systems.
5. **Data Services:** key data services like distributed file systems (IPFS, Storj, etc.) of off-chain data referenced by public keys. Read: Get your data from any source, from anywhere in the world. This enables auditing, advanced analytics, machine learning, and dashboarding services for SmartContracts, blockchains, consortia, and regulators.
6. **Management and Operations:** tools for deployment, management, and operations of enterprise systems.

The base of this three-tier stack is the Distributed Ledger Stack (consensus, networking, database, and any other third-party distributed ledger stacks). This means the foundation can be built on Ethereum, Eris, or Unspent Transaction Output (UTXO) implementations such as Hyperledger.

The true middleware layer involves distributed ledger gateway services, identity and key services, crypto services, and machine learning and business intelligence services. The nodes supporting this layer can be supported by any location (Azure, AzureStack, private data center, AWS, or others). Soon, full libraries of Cryptlets as well as full SmartContract libraries will be available for purchase—just as we download apps from the Google Play store or the Apple iTunes store today.

There are many health-related applications for the use of Cryptlets and SmartContracts. For example, if a medical company determined how to access and populate an anonymized private store of medical information for researchers, it could create a PatientNameless SmartContract and place it on the marketplace, e.g., Apple iTunes store. Then a research group could select a PatientAccessRequest SmartContract to populate data for its next research study. The team that's hired to create the application (inclusive of populated data and machine learning, wrapped with business intelligence) could choose a PatientForResearch Cryptlet that meets or exceeds requirements for the research application.

The top layer is the application layer, where most of the current industry solutions reside.

WHAT'S NEXT?

Many of blockchain's challenges are solved, and most are not integrated into consortium solutions but exist siloed, back to where we started. Some challenges remain outstanding such as self-sovereignty (self-ownership of identity), scalability (off-chain), and interoperability (seamless interaction between systems).

Solving these challenges may be that last stone to uncover a truly collaborative economy—a global economy that shares data.

Mobile Capabilities in Blocks

The corporate fascination with mobile rapid application development has turned to embracing smart contracts. Blockchain applications and functional tools to build ecosystems are growing at lightning speed.

The Ethereum Blockchain as a Service (ETH BaaS) provided by Microsoft Azure and ConsenSys allows customers to create private, public, and consortium-based blockchain environments. The framework provides the foundation to add capabilities such as Cortana Analytics (machine learning), Power BI (data visualization tools), Azure Active Directory (identity and access management for the Cloud), Office 365 (Office online), and CRMOL (CRM Online for Government). New development frameworks will ignite blockchain applications over the next few years.

ETHEREUM BLOCKCHAIN AS A SERVICE ON AZURE

In late 2015, Marley Gray announced a partnership with ConsenSys to offer an Ethereum Blockchain as a Service (EBaaS) on Azure.[3] ConsenSys Ethereum works off four core technological pieces that are coordinated to enable the Ethereum decentralized application platform:

1. **Cryptographic tokens and addresses:** a mathematically secure unique voucher system that can be used to pay for goods, services, or assets, or represent a pseudonymous identity.
2. **Peer-to-peer networking:** individual users connect their computers together, forming a network to exchange data without a central server.
3. **Consensus formation algorithm:** this algorithm permits users of the blockchain to reach consensus about the current state of the blockchain.
4. **Turing complete virtual machine:** a virtual machine is a computer that exists as software, and "Turing complete" means this software computer can run any computer program.

More information is available at the ConsenSys Ethereum website. These core functions were abbreviated for simplicity.[4]

Large Enterprises Finding Little Ones

What can be achieved with Microsoft's blockchain development platforms that's practical? In April 2016, Gem partnered with Philips Healthcare for a blockchain healthcare initiative leveraging Ethereum. Gem is building a blockchain ecosystem for healthcare to address clinical data, claims processing, pharmaceutical supply chains, internet of health, universal health identities, and genomic data management. In January 2016, Gem received an additional $7.1 million in Series A funding, bringing its cumulative funding to $10.4 million. Several investors got in early to support Gem, including Pelion Venture Partners with KEC Ventures, Blockchain Capital, Digital Currency Group, RRE Ventures, Tamarisk Global, Drummond Road Capital, Tekton Ventures, Amplify. LA, Danmar Capital, and James Joaquin.

While Gem was founded in 2014, Philips was founded in 1891. Philips closed Q4 2015 reporting $12.01 billion in sales across its personal care, health and wellness, and domestic appliances businesses. Philips began its 2015 strategy early. By starting in late 2014, Philips had already established the Royal Philips (HealthTech) operating model to take advantage of an aggressive HealthTech. In the 2015 fourth-quarter results presentation, Philips said its objective was to target the $154-billion (CAGR 4 to 10 percent for the period 2014-2018) addressable market across six health opportunities based on the compound annual growth rate (CAGR) of each opportunity:

- Healthy living ($38 billion, CAGR 4%)
- Prevention ($17 billion, CAGR >10%)
- Diagnosis ($39 billion, CAGR 6%)
- Treatment ($17 billion, CAGR 7%)
- Home care ($17 billion, CAGR >10%)
- Monitoring, informatics, and connected care ($28 billion, CAGR 4%)

Gem isn't alone and has strong competition from Bitalo, Bit-Go, Block.io, Blocktrail, and QuickWallet. The challenge for many companies considering exploring blockchain is that many blockchain companies appear very similar. Cursory research yields a blur in value across blockchain companies.

However, further investigation offers a different vantage point once the infrastructure and capabilities are understood— many of the core capabilities among blockchain companies differ wildly.

ETHER.CAMP

The Blockchain as a Service on Microsoft Azure promotes an initial offering of two tools empowering SmartContract-based applications: Ether.Camp, an integrated developer environment[5]; and BlockApps, private and semi-private Ethereum blockchain environment that can deploy into the public Ethereum environment.[6]

Ether.Camp, founded by Roman Mandeleil, does three things well. First, the Ether.Camp team built a Java implementation of Ethereum. Second, they created a well-designed Ether.camp Blockchain Explorer. The Explorer has similar functionality to blockchain.info, but it's akin to an enhanced 2.0 version, allowing users to drill down through smart contracts and even trace code on the blockchain. And third, it offers a straightforward, Integrated Development Environment (IDE), allowing developers to play and deploy. Want to build an app that uses the blockchain for a receipt confirmation? Your team's developers could use this application to do just that.

BLOCKAPPS

BlockApps, short for the "BlockApps STRATO Ethereum Blockchain Network," started with the idea that businesses need blockchain applications, not just blockchains.

The BlockApps platform was designed to allow many-to-many microservices supported by REST APIs (allowing access to legacy systems) to be reinforced with modular architecture and presented under a managed solution. The heart of the system is to promote the rapid deployment and management of blockchain applications. Seamless deployments allow developers to create proofs of concept in a test environment and then deploy to production with no additional development. Many of the products today used for rapid mobile development such as Angular.io, OutSystems Platform, Salesforce, Mendix, Django, and Spring Boot don't offer support for blockchain smart contracts. It's inevitable these industry leaders are racing to incorporate blockchain smart contract functionality into their platforms.

THE FUTURE DIRECTION

From Microsoft with BlockApps on Azure to Stratis, companies are exploring how to develop application frameworks that enable active development across systems (Ethereum and Bitcoin) while offering compatibility. Over the next year, we'll be seeing more blockchain decentralized app hosting offerings with one-click deployment frameworks leveraging managed hosting solutions to achieve scalability and speed.

*"Nothing that has value, real value, has no cost.
Not freedom, not food, not shelter, not healthcare."*

— DEAN KAMEN

CHAPTER 5

HEALTHCARE INTEROPERABILITY

Blockchain, as a foundational technology, is going to revolutionize healthcare and the method by which every patient interacts with healthcare institutions.

Can blockchain technology be used to store electronic medical records securely? The answer to this question depends on the challenge of electronic medical record interoperability between payers and providers, which we must still solve.

The Health Information Technology for Economic and Clinical Health (HITECH) Act, was enacted under Title XIII of the American Recovery and Reinvestment Act of 2009 (Pub.L. 111–5) and was signed into law on February 17, 2009, to promote the adoption and meaningful use of health information technology.

Overall, it's widely accepted that the HITECH Act, as a policy, was a success. It's not surprising, given that the percentage of United States hospitals using digital records skyrocketed from 9.4 percent to 75.5 percent between 2008 and 2014. However, as we inject the patient experience into the definition of success, perspectives change. Providers and payers aren't accountable for interoperability under HITECH. The result has been a fragmented national healthcare system that only hurts the patients we're trying to help.

Interoperability is a monumental challenge that's rarely discussed nationally and needs to be confronted before costs are driven down to open access and allow providers to explore models for improved quality of patient care.

We'll elaborate on how blockchain technology can be applied to electronic medical records by:

1. Providing an overview of blockchain technology
2. Explaining why blockchain technology will change the healthcare industry
3. Discussing how blockchain can affect patient care management

Blockchains Create Trust

What is a blockchain? The blockchain is a series of connected machines for creating trust, according to the Economist Magazine.[1] According to experts on cryptocurrency economy from O'Reilly, in a 2015 article, "Understanding the Blockchain," five foundational concepts of blockchain have been identified:

1. **Decentralized consensus:** on or off Bitcoin's blockchain
2. **Blockchains:** and blockchain services
3. **Smart contracts:** and smart property
4. **Trusted computing:** or trustless transactions
5. **Proof of work:** and proof of stake[2]

Blockchain addresses the previous legitimate concerns of security, scalability, and privacy of electronic medical records. Below is a simple example of how blockchain applied to healthcare works in practice:

- **Patient:** The patient is given a code (private key or hash) and an address that provides the codes to unlock their patient data. While the patient data isn't stored in the blockchain, the blockchain provides the authentication or required hashes (multisignatures, also referred to as multisigs) to be used to enable access to the data (identification and authentication).

- **Provider:** Contributors to a patient's medical record (e.g. providers) are given a separate universal signature (codes or hashes or multisigs). These hashes, when combined with the patient's hash, establish the required authentication to unlock the patient's data.
- **Profile:** Then the patient defines, in their profile, the access rules required to unlock their medical record.
- **Access:** If the patient defines 2-of-2 codes, two separate computer machines (the hashes) would have to be compromised to gain unauthorized access to the data. (In this case, establishing unauthorized, privileged access becomes very difficult when the machine types differ, operating systems differ, and are hosted with different providers.)

Why is this approach more secure than how medical records are stored today?

AN OLD SECURITY PARADIGM

Cybersecurity experts are quietly changing their approach to security. What you know and value about security prevention is eroding. The federal government's HR department learned the hard way. You don't have to.

You probably won't believe this. The new approach to enterprise security is tectonic; traditional virus protection software isn't required. You can stop doing your daily enterprise updates of new virus definitions. The premise that antivirus software is useful in the identification and removal of unauthorized software is flawed. Now, a new paradigm of prevention-based incident response is being introduced that's changing the prevailing security frameworks. First, let's uncover the underbelly of a paradigm.

Thomas Kuhn's famous book, *The Structure of Scientific Revolutions*, changed scientific thinking and introduced the concept of a "paradigm shift." He shared his view that "men whose research is based on shared paradigms are committed to the same rules and standards." Whether we're speaking of concrete scientific achievements, emerging theories, or traditional paradigms, old beliefs can slow progress. What's particularly of interest is Kuhn's viewpoint that a shift can't occur using full communication, forced logic, or neutral experience. Rather, this uprooting must occur all at once. In other words, you can't be "half in" when it comes to adoption.

Past, present, and future belief systems rest on a bedrock of paradigms—beliefs that are internalized by the practitioners who study their effects. Several paradigms were entrenched societal belief systems—until they were changed. We're familiar with many of the past paradigms:

- The Earth is flat.
- The speed of sound may not be exceeded.
- The poles of the Earth are stable.
- It's not possible to split an atom.
- Steel is solid.
- Consciousness is inside our brain.

It's often intriguing to pontificate about modern quantum physics and unified field theory and the design of future paradigms:

- There are universes inside of universes.
- Everything is a "fractal."
- Everything that's happening is in the past.

In this modern world, we wrestle with existing paradigms that are accepted—if not overtly then by limited attempts to prove the alternative.

Expanded value requires expanding thinking. The U.S. Office of Personnel Management (OPM) data breach presents a transferable case relevant to every CIO responsible for organizational security—a practical case that presents a lesson and has a clear solution.

The OPM data breach resulted in personnel records (4.2 million), background checks (21.5 million), and fingerprint records (5.6 million) being exfiltrated from OPM, undetected. OPM had traditional antivirus software running. It didn't help.

This threat went undetected until 2015 (not a typo). Records from current, former, and prospective federal employees were compromised from a system called Standard Form 86, or "SF-86." The template for the SF-86 form is 127 pages, and most applications require additional pages. This system contained detailed lists of federal and military personnel going back 30 years.

To emphasize the significant harm of this breach to national security, Pace provided one example. He noted that special operatives weren't listed in the database. Imagine that there were 15 personnel stationed at a foreign embassy. Twelve are listed in the database. Who are the other three? It wouldn't take long to identify the special operatives with this information.

The OPM data breach leaked our country's most sensitive information, including the identity of anyone employed in a "national security sensitive position." The data exfiltration encompassed a wide range of personnel at all federal agencies, from employees to contractors. The magnitude of this breach was massive.

New tactics are required to thwart security threats — the old antivirus paradigm is no longer effective.

A NEW SECURITY PARADIGM

Prevention-based incident response uses artificial intelligence to identify threats, dispelling the foundational belief that antivirus software is required.

Are you thinking, "Well, that just can't be." I'd kindly draw your attention to the past paradigms that were staples of belief — until they weren't. I didn't say it would be easy. Changing your core belief system is difficult.

Enterprises primarily use antivirus software and run quick scans on endpoints daily if not hourly. Each of us has been on the receiving end of these "quick scans" that are supposed to run at 3 a.m. but somehow kick off during that critical meeting at 9 a.m.

OK, back to the OPM breach. CylancePROTECT is a product that focuses on the prevention of attacks before they ever cause harm. CylancePROTECT predicts, prevents, and protects enterprise endpoints from known and unknown threats by using artificial intelligence, removing the requirement for traditional signature updates.

Cylance takes a mathematical approach to identify malware using machine learning techniques instead of reactive signatures, blocking threats in real time.

A DLL file was ultimately found masked as a McAfee antivirus executable (OPM doesn't use McAfee antivirus software). For over two years, OPM was infected with malware while data was exfiltrated from OPM databases. How does OPM plug this breach? How many endpoints points are affected? Think for a moment: How long would it take your organization to respond to and address every endpoint in your infrastructure—days, months, years?

Cylance was engaged to evaluate 10,000 endpoints and discovered 2,000 pieces of malware and contained the entire breach in 10 days. The result was nothing short of spectacular. The analysis was conducted within 48 hours, and the entire formal report was delivered in one week.

After the Cylance analysis was completed, a law enforcement entity performed a detailed incident response that spanned three months; they found nothing additional.

Embrace prevention-based incident-response approaches that utilize artificial intelligence to identify known and unknown threats—threats with no published signatures.

Prevention-based incident response is a new security paradigm that utilizes artificial intelligence and machine learning to predict threats, prevent attacks, and protect enterprise environments. A new security paradigm has arrived.

Part of the allure of being a CIO is that, as leaders, we learn new concepts daily and have the good fortune to share exceptional ideas with our organizations. This paradigm shift is one of those exceptional ideas. It's worth your attention.

HOW DOES BLOCKCHIN IMPROVE SECURITY?

Would these data breaches have occurred if two separate computers needed to be compromised to gain access? How about five computers or 100 computers?

Today, blockchain has what's called M-of-N multisignature (multisig), meaning multisignatures are required to establish the authentication required to unlock data (likely stored in the Cloud). The M-of-N multisig means that 'N' computers would all be required (multiple computer hashes combined) to decrypt the code, e.g. providing the authentication to access that patient's medical records. For example, an M-of-5 means that five machines would have to be compromised, each with separately controlled codes or hashes. There are also other variants; for example, 2-of-3 multisig, which means not only would two separate codes be required but the patient data could still be unlocked even if only two of the three keys were available. For example, if the three keys were held by a patient's physician, spouse, and a neighbor, two of the three keys would be needed to unlock the data (typically used for emergencies involving life-and-death situations).

CONDITIONAL PRIVACY

Privacy is a major concern—until it isn't. For example, if you ask a patient if they'd like to share their full personal health history including blood type, all previous procedures, and life habits with providers, they likely will say no. If you ask a similar question when the patient's heart rate goes below 40 beats per minute (say, in an ambulance), would he or she be willing to share it? They'll be quick to exclaim, "Of course!" Access and consent to medical information is a conditional decision and determined based on environmental context. Today, EHR systems have a difficult time factoring in conditional consent.

Often a patient either authorizes full access to their medical records (all-in) or no access. This model doesn't meet patient needs and will evolve.

The beauty of blockchain technology, applied to healthcare, is a centralized platform that decentralizes health data (medical records), increasing security of sensitive information. A patient can now use their own signature combined with that of a hospital signature to unlock data to provide more secure access to medical information for use in treatment. The patient, by using their profile, has full control of their medical information and can select the information shared and viewed by providers or doctors. This model lifts the costly burden of maintaining a patient's medical histories away from the hospitals: eventually, cost savings will make it full cycle back to the patient receiving care.

Are you still a bit unsure what blockchain is really all about? For now, allow George Howard, Forbes contributor, to frame it for you: "Bitcoin is to the Blockchain as Porn was to the Internet." Blockchain technology is secure, scalable, tamper-proof, and timestamped. Additionally, by removing the central point of failure, it's nearly impossible to "hack" the blockchain.

Healthcare and Industry Tectonic Shifts

The benefits of electronic medical health records are widely known and broadly accepted, adding value to patient care. Excessive costs of managing and maintaining electronic medical record systems impede interoperability. Additionally, when coupled with the lack of payment reform, most financial motivation is removed for payers and providers to be interoperable. Now there's a way to improve transparency, driven by the patient. How do blockchains improve transparency? Reid Williams, the senior designer and engineer at IDEO Futures, argues, "Blockchains offer a way to introduce transparency into supply chains and to create entirely new opportunities for participation."[3] This is important for patient medical history continuity and the medical record chain of care.

ELECTRONIC MEDICAL RECORDS

Blockchains applied to healthcare will solve the interoperability challenge of electronic medical records, where currently there's no coherence at county, state, or national levels, such that global electronic medical record interoperability is nothing short of impossible. Before blockchain, the idea of global electronic medical records was a dream we only hoped our children's children could solve.

Exploring a practical example makes this experience more real.

I'd like to introduce you to Diane. Diane is married, in her mid-50s, works hard, and enjoys life when she can break away from work.

While on the way to work one day, Diane felt a bit lightheaded; but, after her workout, that was often the case. She didn't think any more about it. After she'd arrived at the office, she collapsed. Co-workers scrambled to call 911, EMTs arrived and scanned her PatientChainID (similar to a national patient identifier). Diane, similar to most patients, had a profile set up previously.

The profile Diane had set up, with help from her primary care doctor, included rules and identified family members that could approve access to her medical records in the case of an emergency. Diane had three family members listed including her husband, Jake. The EMT announced and requested access to Diane's medical records on the PatientChain Network.

Within minutes, Jake had verified access, and the EMT was able to access Diane's medical records. The EMTChainID and the HospitalChainID, when combined with Diane's PatientChainID (authorized by Jake), unlocked Diane's medical records, which enabled the EMTs to provide more specific care, considering her pre-existing conditions.

Diane was diagnosed with syncope (pronounced SIN-ko-pee), defined as a sudden, brief loss of consciousness and posture caused by decreased blood flow to the brain. She'd fainted due to low blood sugar. According to Web-MD, fainting is a common problem, accounting for 3 percent of emergency room visits and 6 percent of hospital admissions.

Diane was held for the day and released that evening. A month later, Diane reviewed her profile (who she'd verified/approved to access her medical records) and she removed the hospital and the EMT, since that access was no longer required. Diane had an electronic medical record that was accessible on a cloud-based network, globally, by any payer and any provider after authorization is provided.

Diane, of course, is imaginary and now fully recovered.

GLOBAL HEALTHCARE INTEROPERABILITY

Interoperability and payment reform are the two toughest obstacles in the quest toward improving healthcare. Bitcoin is only one example in a sea of blockchain potential applications: we can't forget its application to healthcare. Blockchain may well be a game changer. Whether the digital currency industry takes off or not, blockchain technology will revolutionize every industry and the ways consumers and patients interact.

Let's start by transforming the patient experience. Let's start by believing we'll live in a healthier tomorrow. If enough of us believe, we might just change the provision of global healthcare and truly solve the problem of medical record interoperability.

"Remember, a dead fish can float down a stream,
but it takes a live one to swim upstream."

— W.C. FIELDS

CHAPTER 6

GOVERNMENT'S BLOCKCHAIN PLAY

Propagated by experts, industry veterans spanning every facet of the healthcare ecosystem is the myth that healthcare interoperability is impossible.

These experts would have us believe that the United States healthcare system so complex that healthcare interoperability is a fantasy that will never be achieved.

The National Institute of Standards and Technology (NIST), in partnership with the Office of the National Coordinator for Health Information Technology (ONC), launched a request for papers called the ONC Blockchain Challenge. The ONC was looking to explore the "use of blockchain in Health IT and Health released Research."

The New Definition of Healthcare Interoperability

In 2013, the Healthcare Information and Management Systems Society (HIMSS) defined healthcare interoperability as:

> the ability of different information technology systems and software applications to communicate, exchange data, and use the information that has been exchanged.

This definition is alluring but inaccurate and incomplete. I'd like to offer this updated definition:

> Healthcare interoperability is the ability of multiple healthcare ecosystems to work in harmony without unreasonable efforts by the ecosystems' producers and consumers.

Healthcare has a track record of forgetting the patient. Interoperability is a societal problem that involves organizations *and* technology, not just technology.

Healthcare patient data interoperability is critical to enabling access, improving quality, and decreasing the cost of care. William Dailey, MD, practicing physician and chief of medical information at Golden Valley Memorial Healthcare in Clinton, Missouri, and I co-authored a paper and submitted it to the ONC Blockchain Challenge. The paper explores how to close the gap among providers and their desire to have accurate patient medical information for clinical diagnosis.

The ONC and NIST Partnership

The ONC and NIST partnered on this initiative, but why? Understanding both the ONC and NIST organizational missions can help justify the logical alignment for them jointly supporting the ONC Blockchain Challenge. The ONC is the primary federal entity coordinating nationwide efforts to implement and use the most advanced health information technology and the electronic exchange of health information. It's responsible for national healthcare interoperability. NIST is a measurement-standards laboratory and a nonregulatory agency of the United States Department of Commerce. Its mission is to promote innovation and industrial competitiveness.

Many leaders in information technology associate NIST with 800-53 or the NIST Special Publication 800-53, a standards document that recommends security controls for federal information systems and organizations. However, NIST's mission extends further. NIST is organized into laboratory programs that include Nanoscale Science and Technology, Engineering, Information Technology, Neutron Research, Material Measurement, and Physical Measurement. The alignment of the ONC with NIST is an interesting partnership and signals to industry that security and policy are coupled. Together, these two organizations have the potential to create a secure national standard for healthcare interoperability.

FHIR Gets Us Close

Our paper, the second one I submitted to the challenge, is titled "Micro-Identities Improve Healthcare Interoperability With Blockchain: Deterministic Methods for Connecting Patient Data to Uniform Patient Identifiers,"[1] and it proposes solutions to the ongoing concerns regarding healthcare interoperability in the United States.

The topic of healthcare interoperability affects every patient in the United States. This Blockchain Challenge encourages a nation to think about solutions, not just expound on the problems.

Our paper on micro-identities examines how this new healthcare ecosystem will interoperate. Global experts in bioinformatics believe a solution exists and that we, as a society, must not stop searching for it.

Gil Alterovitz, Harvard Medical School professor in the school's Division of Medical Sciences, core faculty member at the Computational Health Informatics Program at Boston Children's Hospital, and co-chair of Health Level Seven International (HL7) Clinical Genomics Work Group, said he found the paper insightful and a necessary step in exploring options toward a national healthcare interoperability solution. Alterovitz stated,

I found the temporal, geospatial use for identification to be an interesting little nugget. I don't think I have seen that before explicitly called out as a feature—where the patient would use the previous location in helping make an ID. On another hand, its practicality is a question mark—time will tell. Also, it is one of the first pieces out there linking blockchain to implementation via FHIR.[2]

Founded in 1987, Health Level Seven International (HL7) formed a not-for-profit organization dedicated to providing comprehensive standards for electronic health information to support the delivery of health services. Leveraging this framework for integration among providers is straightforward. The HL7 Fast Healthcare Interoperability Resources (FHIR, pronounced "Fire") standard is faster to learn, develop, and implement. Also, the framework is free. It doesn't involve proprietary software or adapters.

Our paper highlights that while the specification is comprehensive, it does have gaps evident during healthcare implementations.

The HL7 FHIR specification will soon be complete and implemented by major electronic medical record (EMR) vendors supported by the Argonaut Project. At that time, each healthcare entity will have RESTful interface(s) with the information they choose to make available to trusted partners, accessible by way of their HL7 FHIR server(s); however, specific gaps exist in locating the appropriate server, obtaining entity trust, and requesting co-located patient information at the next point of care (POC). Patient demographics such as date of birth, gender, country, zip code, ethnicity, and blood type may be slightly different due to multiple factors and therefore prevent acquisition of the correct data. Identifying the patient correctly is essential to care.

Blockchain technology has the potential to address these technology gaps. Novel methods for identity verification and sharing healthcare event transactions between entities will advance healthcare stakeholders towards complete solutions.[3]

Our paper describes how the HL7 FHIR flexible framework has the ability to support mobility and mobile health, social media, personal health records, public health, payment systems, and clinical research.

HL7 FHIR provides a needed standard for the clinical sharing of patients' medical information. However, the challenge of matching patient identities among facilities remains unsolved.

IDENTITY MATCHING

Throughout the paper, Dr. Dailey and I explore matching patient identities at Golden Valley Memorial Healthcare in a condition referred to as high sensitivity and low specificity. Sensitivity refers to a test's ability to correctly designate an individual with the disease. A highly sensitive test means there are few false-negative results and thus fewer cases of the disease are missed. The specificity of a test relates to its ability to correctly designate an individual who doesn't have the disease. The process and result are documented in detail within the paper.

This experiment inspired a data test Golden Valley Memorial Healthcare, a small, 50-bed, rural healthcare facility in Missouri using real patient data. Interestingly, the hospital has two, separate yet highly patient-concordant EMR systems (inpatient and ambulatory), making it ripe for analysis. Each EMR system contained approximately 70,000 to 90,000 records.

How would patient matching among facilities work? Allow me to explain.

The result was that John, a sample patient, was verified. The only data viewable by the receptionist is an option to select the date of the visit. Once that's selected, a list of matching locations appeared in a drop-down box. The receptionist performed a verification, allowing all available data to be immediately pulled from all encounters at that facility as a cascade of FHIR queries for patient John.

What's accomplished by this method? This process unlocks healthcare interoperability for the alignment of patient identity, confidentiality, integrity, and accessibility, resulting in better patient outcomes.

The Cryptocitizen: Co-Creation of Trust Using Blockchain

Is it possible to design a crypto-identity for each individual to establish autonomy and ownership of an individual's identity mathematically?

We define the term cryptocitizen and the impact on interoperability by stating that,

> the cryptocitizen [is] a concept of shared societal trust, where citizens have a new relationship with authority, reducing government involvement in decentralization— availability of government services versus citizens being directly governed.[4]

The core framework of interoperability revolves around the cryptocitizen and the idea of self-sovereignty. We explain,

> Self-ownership (or sovereignty of the individual, individual sovereignty, or individual autonomy) is the concept of property in one's own person, expressed as the moral or natural right of a person to have bodily integrity and be the exclusive controller of her or his own body and life. Tilting this definition, we can apply self-ownership to healthcare and ownership of patient information... Self-sovereign identity is guided by the principle that every patient is the source and therefore owner of their own identity.[5]

How does this relate to interoperability? If a provider can't identify a patient, how are the patient's medical records accessed? How does medical information flow among facilities? Today, information doesn't pass seamlessly among healthcare entities. Patients have to request their medical information, and often the transfer of information is inefficient and carried out by fax, email, or the mailing of hard copies.

We presented the argument that self-sovereignty with distributed consensus is an enabler to empower patients to take back control of their medical identities.

> The pinnacle of medical records' interoperability is patient-controlled medical records. With blockchain technologies, patients can own and control their identity, access their data, and conditionally authorize the sharing of medical records with providers.[6]

As healthcare leaders, we have the potential to open the mind of society and introduce the possibility that blockchain frameworks will solve our patient identity problem—achieving national healthcare interoperability.

Exploring Trust Versus Truth for Healthcare

Let's explore one of the three research propositions examined in the paper: trust vs. truth.

> At some point, virtually every health system will be compromised. Healthcare leaders have a duty to verify the integrity of their healthcare systems independently. Today, this is done by adding new security components into the environment, e.g. virus protection software, hard or soft firewalls, virtual private networks, etc. The fundamental assumption in the decision to patch security gaps with hardware or software assumes that components won't be compromised. It's troubling that when transmitting data, it's not possible to determine if new or old components have been compromised. Now, with blockchain, healthcare system administrators can prove the healthcare data hasn't been compromised. This is accomplished by estab-

lishing data authenticity with the chain of custody utilizing blockchain technologies.

The Keyless Signature Infrastructure (KSI) is designed to provide scalable, digital, signature-based authentication for electronic data, machines, and humans. Every healthcare data transfer can be captured and timestamped, creating proof of authenticity and restoring truth into our healthcare system. This paradigm shift offers data integrity and visibility, previously unheard of—moving healthcare toward transparent truth, not trust. KSIs can resolve the lack of consistent methods for conducting patient matching and decrease the occurrence of out-of-date and incorrect patient-matching errors. Leveraging KSI can prevent man-in-the-middle (MiM) attacks. MiM attacks are a process where a user gains unauthorized access to communications between two parties who believe they're directly communicating with each other. When applied to healthcare, MiM attacks can alter valid matches, resulting in unauthorized users consuming the data for unknown and potential nefarious purposes, manufacturing 'no matches found' despite the availability of valid matches. KSI helps to ensure data integrity and authenticity, protecting the patient.[7]

Healthcare can utilize blockchain technology to provide a nationally shared healthcare resource. This resource will enable patient identity matching, identity linking, redundant connectivity, location, and the retrieval of granular patient data to and from any EMR.

Blockchain Leapfrogs Patient Identity Matching

It's time to move past theoretical results and engage in practical research exploring the use of blockchain technologies for autonomous monitoring of medical devices. We, as a society, have to believe in something, and if we're going to invest the time, then working toward improving the health of a nation is a noble first step.

Blockchain technologies will enable patient identity matching.

A lot has been written covering blockchain and healthcare over the past year, from articles on blockchain applications for healthcare to blog posts by healthcare industry experts exploring blockchain technology as the solution for healthcare interoperability.

THE STARTUP FRENZY FORGOT ABOUT HEALTHCARE

The world is talking about uses of blockchain in the financial services industry. This seems reasonable, given that there have been over one billion dollars invested in blockchain startups.

The majority of these investments have been within the financial sector. The cumulative investment in blockchain is likely double the above forecasted investment amount. Several of the stealth-mode startup companies were funded with pre-seed or seed money and, to date, are staying well under the radar.

However, many startups are eager to get noticed and have published formal press releases. These companies include Brave, Coinigy, Netki, Circle Internet Financial, Mediachain, TechBureau, Fluent, bitFlyer, Ethcore, Tibit, BitKan, Custos Media Technologies, Bitwala, Bitt, Stratumn, Rootstock, Elliptic, Chronicled, Keza, Loyyal, Chainalysis, Simplex, SurBTC, Blockstream, SatoshiPay, Digital Asset Holdings, Gem, and Zebpay.

The focus has been on the financial markets and private startups; only two companies have anything to do with healthcare and only two startups are primarily concentrating on applying blockchain to healthcare: Gem, of Venice, California; and Clinical Blockchain, of Philadelphia. We need to use what we have in blockchain basics and start to dive into real solutions to unearth the root causes of healthcare interoperability in the United States.

MICRO-IDENTITIES FOR BETTER PATIENT CARE

Patients, to the surprise of many, only visit their primary care physicians 54.6 percent of the time when they visit a doctor. Where do they go for the other 45.4 percent? If they go to another doctor, the latter would have no access to the patient's historical medical records.

Do different providers' patient management systems talk to one another? How are clinical treatments shared? What's the process flow to move administrative and billing information to payers? In the United States, the care experience isn't integrated; each integration is a one-off.

The goal of the triple aim is pretty straightforward:

1. Improve the patient experience of care (including quality and satisfaction)
2. Improve the health of populations
3. Reduce the per capita cost of healthcare

Unfortunately, progress has been limited, and national healthcare costs are on the rise. Shared-cost and inventive distributed decentralized solutions offer a way out.

The drive behind this paper is to present a hybrid model that integrates the FHIR interoperability standards describing data formats and elements. This model also includes an application programming interface (API) for exchanging electronic health records using blockchain technologies for better patient access to health information.

HL7 FHIR, the Primer for Healthcare Interoperability

Our paper provides an overview of HL7 FHIR and identifies it as a critical piece of the solution to healthcare interoperability.

Fast Healthcare Interoperability Resources (HL7 FHIR) is a draft standard describing data formats and elements (known as 'resources') and an Application Programming Interface (API) for exchanging Electronic health records... The HL7 FHIR specification allows secure information exchange and is a positive step toward interoperability. HL7 FHIR separates the data structure from the wider problem of entity-to-entity trust, centralized server broadcasting, and patient identification and matching spanning entities.[8]

Less is more. This adage is true of patient matching: the more discreet items you try to match, the less likely they are to match. Keying errors, pseudonyms, misspellings and the like, impact the conformability of patient data. Also, poor data quality results in searches with no data matches. Successful matching strategies are a proprietary mix of deterministic and stochastic or probabilistic methods. They are proprietary for numerous reasons, which are beyond the scope of this paper. Stochastic methods are commonly used to overcome poor data quality.[9]

Wayne Kubick, the Chief Technology Officer at HL7, is responsible for advancing the organization's mission and strategic plans. After reading the paper that Dr. Dailey and I co-authored, Kubick added his perspective,

This paper presents a wealth of information on using technology for healthcare, and clearly, the topic of exploring Blockchain with the HL7 FHIR standard is worthy of much additional research as a potential path forward toward improving interoperability.[10]

Gem's founder and CEO, Micah Winkelspecht, is bullish about blockchain and the potential to improve healthcare outcomes. A visionary who founded Gem in 2014, Winkelspecht launched Gem as a blockchain application platform to transform the way companies, and industries connect to solve impossible problems.

Gem is one of the few blockchain companies strategically positioned to accelerate healthcare outcomes, grounded by a foundational application platform. Winkelspecht has proven his ability to forecast technology adapting to new market conditions. After reading the paper that Dr. Dailey and I co-authored, Winkelspecht had this to say:

> This paper does a great job of capturing the largest opportunities for blockchains in healthcare. Nichol and Dailey correctly identify the big killer app for a healthcare blockchain: a patient-centric, tamper-proof, comprehensive medical history tied to a global, self-sovereign patient ID. Blockchains will solve some of the largest problems around privacy, security, and availability of health information as it is exchanged across patients, providers, payers, researchers, and even governments.

The future of healthcare and innovation will be led by the innovators bold enough to believe in better patient outcomes.

Framework for Healthcare Interoperability

There's a lot of talk about blockchain for healthcare but there are very few frameworks that provide a reference to explain the concepts. The paper Dr. Dailey and I co-authored communicates a framework to explain interactions required for efficient blockchain-supported care systems:

> The below interoperability strategic healthcare framework establishes a model for incorporating blockchain technologies into healthcare.

> Accessible healthcare data that's open-sourced but siloed will transition to healthcare interoperability where ubiq-

uitous access to data will be secure and ever-present. In this new healthcare environment, patients will be able to audit each other's behavior mutually, obtaining provable security of patient health information.[11]

*"Don't worry about people stealing your ideas.
If your ideas are any good, you'll have to ram them
down people's throats."*

— HOWARD AIKEN

CHAPTER 7

THE DISTRIBUTED WEB: IPFS

s IPFS the future? And what exactly is it? IPFS (interplanetary file system) is a peer-to-peer, hypermedia protocol to make the Web faster, safer, and more open. IPFS provides historical versioning (like Git) and powers the creation of diversely resilient networks that enable persistent availability with or without Internet backbone connectivity. When looking up files, you're asking the network to find nodes storing the content behind a unique hash. Most importantly, every file can be found by human-readable names using a decentralized naming system called IPNS (interplanetary naming system).

Each file and all of the blocks within it are given a unique fingerprint called a cryptographic hash. IPFS removes duplications across the network and tracks version history for every file. Each network node stores only content it's interested in along with some indexing information that helps figure out who's storing what. [For more information, IPFS has an excellent whitepaper that explains the peer-to-peer, distributed file system with the vision of connecting all computing devices with the same system of records.[1]]

Everything of value involves data. Where data lives and how it's accessed is about to change. The Internet of Data Structures (IoDS) is emerging as one of the most significant advancements in data within the last decade and is transforming the Web from linking data by location to linking data with hashes. Is your organization prepared?

HTTP (the Hypertext Transfer Protocol) is the foundation of communication on the World Wide Web. Hypertext is structured text that enables us to access content throughout the Web using logical links (hyperlinks) between nodes containing data. But what if HTTP were no longer needed? What if there were a better way to communicate and connect data. That better way is IPFS.

URLs are out; hashes are in.

Unpacking the Permanent Web

IoDS has arrived for healthcare. IPFS, combined with blockchain, creates a new layer of the Internet. Is your business exploring it?

How do you determine if your organization is designing innovative experiences? There's a simple question that provides that answer: "Is your organization talking about IPFS?" If the answer is yes, you're likely relevant to the healthcare innovation discussion. If, however, the answer is no, your organization missed the innovation bus.

IPFS is a foundational technology that will transform healthcare by 2025.

The Fix for Medical Record Link Rot

P2P file sharing is fun and easy. IPFS holds power to create a P2P network of medical records—easy to share and access. We'll explore why P2P file sharing can impact how medical information is shared.

What to do about the problem of medical record link rot in healthcare? What is link rot? Link rot is the process by which hyperlinks on individual websites or the Internet in general point to web pages, servers, or other resources that have become permanently unavailable.

Medical information is out there, but getting access proves difficult. Getting access to your unified medical profile—in which patients are required to collect pieces of their medical profiles sprinkled across the country—sits well outside the level of acceptable frustration.

The lack of interoperability affects patients. IPFS presents a new approach for connecting information—a potential fix for medical record link rot.

A Napster for Healthcare

BitTorrent, LimeWire (gasp), Napster, FastTrack, eDonkey, Gnutella, and Vuze were among the many famous, open-source, peer-to-peer (P2P) clients or products supporting file sharing. BitTorrent and Gnutella enable the downloading of any files. Using these, clients could swap videos, music, and software files over the Internet.

Napster was, however, a centralized model in which peer computers would register with the core central server and provide their file-sharing lists. Peers then sent queries to the central server, which retained a master index of all available files. The central server connected the query computer to a peer (with the requested files).

The strength of this approach was that the central server always knew where the files were located, searching was fast and efficient, and the answers were guaranteed to be correct. The challenge with the Napster model (aside from the obvious one we all know about) was that it depended on a centralized server, which resulted in a single point of failure. The problem was magnified because the centralized server needed to have adequate computing power to handle all queries—a setup that could have resulted in unreliable service if not appropriately scaled.

P2P Sharing for a Healthier Tomorrow

The limitations associated with centralized servers spawned the emergence of Gnutella. Developed by Justin Frankel and Tom Pepper of Nullsoft shortly after Nullsoft's acquisition by

AOL, Gnutella was the first, major, P2P client. This is where the story takes a turn.

The original developers announced the launch on Slashdot, but AOL stopped it over legal concerns. Thousands had already downloaded the decentralized, peer-to-peer network client, the protocol was reverse-engineered, and open-source clones quickly surfaced across the Internet. AOL later did release the source code under a GNU General Public License (GPL).[2]

Why does the P2P sharing of information matter? Today, one reason records can't be shared is due to the multiple systems, databases, and formats in which medical information is stored. A P2P approach to healthcare would inch us closer to a unified medical record system—accessible by heterogeneous systems.

IPFS allows distributed access to medical records by heterogeneous systems using the same file structures.

The Movement from HTTP to IPFS

Let's step a layer deeper into how the IPFS structure is designed, and I'll offer an introduction to the IPFS stack.

Where does IPFS fit into our existing infrastructure? How do you communicate the value of this technology and its application in business transformation? Those questions are exactly what we'll tackle.

HTTP uses hyperlinks that translate into locations to connect discrete objects and data sets. IPFS is like HTTP, but instead of using locations provided by a group of servers, IPFS uses a peer-to-peer network to share context using hash values or hashes. In IPFS, content is addressable using hashes—the hashed value of the content.

IPFS is a Merkle-addressed transport protocol for distributed data structures. The IPFS stack breaks down into three general buckets, each offering its own particular value:

1. **Using the data:** applications (the IPFS stack)[3]
2. **Defining the data:** naming, Merkle-DAG (IPNS,[4] IPLD)[5]
3. **Moving the data:** exchanges, routing, network (Libp2p)[6]

These three primary buckets further divide into five broad categories that comprise the infrastructure stack:

1. **Applications:** Etherpad, VLC, Git, Ethereum, and Whisper
2. **Naming:** DNS, IPNS, EthNames, Namecoin, or IPLD
3. **Exchange:** BitTorrent, Bitswap, FTP, HTTP
4. **Routing:** Gossip, Chord, Kad DHT, mDNS, Delegated, I2P and TOR
5. **Network:** CJDNS, UDT, uTP, WebRTC, QUIC, TCP, WebSockets, I2P and TOR

Building the Internet of Data Structures (IoDS)

Identities ensure that connected peers exchange public keys. The public and private keys are encrypted with a passphrase. The Network addresses the transport protocol, network reliability, connectivity, integrity, and authenticity (checking sender's public key). The Routing ensures peers can find other peers and determines which peers can serve other peers (technically, using a distributed sloppy hash table—DSHT—based on S/Kademlia and Coral). The Exchange sends and receives blocks of distributed data with a BitTorrent-inspired protocol called the BitSwap protocol. The Objects sit above the distributed hash table and BitSwap (a peer-to-peer system for storing and distributing blocks quickly). The Merkle-DAG links objects connected by cryptographic hashes of the targets embedded in the sources.

Much of this functionality is available using Git data structures, but Merkle-DAGs offer the added benefits of context addressing (including links), tamper resistance, and de-duplication.

The Files are a set of objects (block of data, list of blocks, tree of collections, and commits—version history snapshots). The Naming ensures that objects are permanent and can be retrieved by their hash, among other properties. Lastly, Applications can run over the Internet and leverage the principles and features of IPFS to create a web of Merkle-links connecting data (objects and blocks) for business applications.

Why does any of this matter? Any change, update, or tweak would be listed in order. Patients could be informed and have access to every addition to their personal medical record—a historical, longitudinal medical record that's never misplaced.

Accessing Files on IPFS

It's easier to understand IPFS if we frame it next to concepts we're already familiar with, like DNS.

The example below of HTTP shows a typical website URL for a company logo and the host name translated into an IP address using DNS. Next is the IPFS example for comparison, which uses the IPNS and IPFS working together. IPNS allows the storage of a reference to an IPFS hash under the namespace of your peerID (the hash of your public key). This IPFS hash references an addressable object in IPFS using a hash value that points to a hash object linked to another hash object until your destination is found.

IPFS also achieves immutability by separating key management from file system security.[7] The filenames contain public keys, making them self-certifying pathnames. Public key hashes resolve pointers that are signed with a private key to access content.

HTTP

http://**peterbnichol.com**/linktohash/logo.jpeg
(domain name service)
http://**10.11.12.13**/linktohash/logo.jpeg (IP address)

IPFS

/ipns/**ReE45fRer5LR3**/linktohash/logo.jpeg
(InterPlanetary name service - optional)
/ipfs/**ReE78kGrd5KJ2**/linktohash/logo.jpeg (hash address)

The process of linking by objects is similar to how inodes operate, except hash values are used. An inode is a data structure on a file system that stores all the information about a file except its name and its actual data.

Posting Content with IPFS

IPFS offers a unique approach to addressing and moving content within a network. If peers were uninterested in your content, the standard, paid, backup solutions (AWS, Azure, Swarm) could be leveraged. Also, unlike other peer-to-peer distributed networks, IPFS only downloads explicitly required data. IPFS does not pull full copies of data.

Publishing content to IPFS is similar to publishing content through a private blockchain. It's also possible to distribute content on IPFS and then remove yourself as a host who serves that content (in theory, removing the need for infrastructure?). Here's an example of posting data in an IPFS world:

1. Create content
2. Generate key names
3. Sign content
4. Distribute to peer-to-peer network
5. Register key name and point to hash of public key

Theoretically, this process removes the need for locally owned and managed infrastructure. In practice, standard, paid, backup services may be required such as those listed above.

What Will Be Impacted?

Any products, services, or interactions that leverage storage or save data have the potential to be affected.

This foundational technology layer will affect where data is stored (traditional databases to IPFS) and how data is accessed (URLs to hashes). Every platform that requires linked and encrypted communications has the potential to benefit from IPFS.

Dapps and mobile applications will quietly shift to the Internet of Data Structures as scale and interoperability become increasingly critical.

HTTP routes static traffic to a central server, decreasing the attack surface and making targeted attacks more efficient. In contrast, IPFS is a distributed storage system. Distributed denial-of-service (DDoS) attacks would be harder to execute on platforms running IPFS. By using IPFS and distributing the attack surface across peers, this makes conducting DDoS attacks significantly more difficult because content can be accessed through the distributed storage network.

The Relationships Between IPFS and Blockchain

The alignment of IPFS and blockchain technologies is a natural partnership. Together, the outcome is a powerful, distributed, permanent, digital ledger that's accessible across heterogeneous systems.

IPFS is "the permanent Web." It accomplishes this feat through a combination of distributed, peer-to-peer file system storage and Merkle data structures that enable versioned file systems to communicate. Peers (or nodes) don't need to trust each other.

IPFS provides five main benefits:

1. **Deduplication:** addressing data by hashes, providing integrity, distributed persistence (e.g. removing duplication medical records).
2. **Self-distribution:** removal of dependencies to content distributors (e.g. the payers and providers in healthcare).
3. **Peer-to-peer transfers:** proximal users can share content with each another, reducing bandwidth requirements (e.g., two local hospitals can share information without it being required to go through centralized servers).
4. **Archiving:** immutable data storage and offline data access, similar to Git, that's helpful in low-connectivity environments with weak infrastructures (helpful for immediate, local access to medical histories, for example).
5. **Directory browsing:** faster browsing of data (e.g., quicker searching through medical notes for themes or clinical trends that could impact outcomes).

Blockchain removes—or disintermediates—the middleman from business transactions and, by doing so, improves the value of existing products, services, and interaction. Expanding on our earlier two basic advantages, preventing double spending and achieving consensus, blockchains provide five main benefits:

1. **Disintermediation:** removes the middleman or "go-between" from transactions (e.g., removing healthcare players that aren't adding value).
2. **Empowered consumers:** consumers own their data (for example, patients control who can view and access their medical information).

3. **Data integrity:** a distributed, public (for authorized miners), time-stamped, and persistent list of transactions (every update to medical records is carved in stone; you could add stones but not remove them).

4. **Preventing double spending:** stopping duplicate expenditures of assets (thus curbing the ability to send conflicting medical records).

5. **Establishing consensus:** a network of computers that agree on the state of transactions (providing a single source of truth for your medical history).

Blockchains already have a DAG structure inherent in the protocol that links historical blocks to hash values. One challenge of generic blockchains is the duplication of data supported by blockchain structures. IPFS solves this problem.

A blockchain-state database is a writable stream for applications that consume blocks. This blockchain-state is used to process, in order, blockchain blocks (e.g. for searching the blockchain or a medical wallet). With a traditional blockchain, every transaction needs to be stored. However, using an IPFS foundational blockchain, only the state entries (or changes between two blocks) need to be stored.

The result is a performance gain from deduplication, a simplification of block accessibility, and the formation of a simplified and easier to maintain data structure.

Chain Tagging

Storing information on-chain or off-chain is a frequent debate. The root of this debate centers around whether all data should be stored on-chain or if only the hashes should be stored on-chain. I've yet to meet an individual who doesn't have a clear preference leaning one way or the other on this issue.

Several blockchains, like Ethereum, require miners to pay a fee for blockchain storage. This fee is charged to miners (peers or nodes) that want to commit transactions to the consensus-driven and peer-to-peer distributed ledger. Changing the associated state database requires "proof," which has a cost. This cost is charged back to the miner. The reason for this fee is to limit miners storing non-value-add data or creating "blockchain bloat." To prevent blockchain bloat, large blockchain implementations often choose to store only the hashes on-chain, not the data. This action reduces fees associated with storing data for the associated database-state.

"Chain tagging," or "What's the chain tag?" will soon be as popular as the common phrase, "What's the website link?"

Defining the on-chain or off-chain state for data is critical. IPFS (used as a blockchain-state database) would need to tag each piece of data with either an on-chain or off-chain tag. In this deceptively simple approach, data would be managed off-chain and changes wouldn't require miner intervention. Data would be permanently addressable.

Interestingly, IPFS offers a solution for a permanent, version-controlled file system for data storage. Imagine that the data you have could be linked securely to any other database, system or platform in the world—and never have a broken link—on a global healthcare blockchain.

Healthcare Leaders Should Be Asking Questions About IPFS

We've all been there. We're sitting in a meeting and we hear this sentence: "This technology will transform how we do business." Everyone who's been in technology for more than a year has watched this show. Usually, it's a short production that never makes it to Broadway.

But then there were those few times when we didn't believe, and that fledgling technology was, in fact, transformative. Which side of the table are you going to sit on? The pessimistic side of "we'll wait until it proves itself" or the optimistic side of "let's experiment, explore, and validate the potential." You need to decide for yourself, your team, and your organization.

My 2017 proposal paper, "An e-Government Interoperability Framework to Reduce Waste, Fraud, and Abuse" tackles how to solve interoperability for citizens, businesses, and governments.[8] IPFS and blockchain provide a stabilized foundation for interoperability. IPFS has the potential to create a new layer of the Internet—a layer in which data can be accessed across value-based ecosystems, with industry agnosticism:

1. Government agencies to government agencies
2. Companies to companies
3. Towns to towns
4. Cities to cities
5. States to states
6. Countries to countries

Government agencies, companies, towns, cities, states, and countries could all share data, information, knowledge, and ultimately wisdom. IPFS connects the "web of value."

The problem with healthcare isn't that we don't have enough technology. It's also not an issue of broken processes (of which we have many). The single greatest problem in healthcare is the nonbelievers—people who don't believe, deep down, that transformation is possible.

IPFS will impact every healthcare application deployed by 2020.

The data structures within the healthcare industry that hold our patient and clinical information are going to experience a transformation. The transformation won't be by disruptive technology; it will be by foundational technology. Think about how your business and technical foundations are shifting, and begin.

IPFS: Foundation for the Internet Upgrade

How is data available today within the unstructured swamp of medical information? We have petabytes of individual genomic records that need hosting and real-time media streams to capture. How are these massive data sets going to be linked?

There's no trust between nodes, and there's no single point of failure. Does this sound like something we need in healthcare? Applying IPFS to the storing of medical information would mean no trust requirement among providers and no single point of failure to prevent patients from accessing their medical records.

Merkle trees or hash trees are a core tenet of why blockchains add value.[9] Merkle trees are a structure in which every nonleaf node is labeled with the hash of the labels or the values (leaves) of its child nodes. Huh? Each branch or link is dependent upon the previous branch, similar to a branch of a tree and its leaves.

Not familiar with hashes or Merkle trees? Not to worry. We'll explore IPFS and its impact and macro principles to create a new spiderweb of connections on top of the Internet.

IPFS is a global, distributed file system that forms a generalized Merkle-DAG, a directed acyclic graph whose objects are linked to each other (usually just by their cryptographic hash—a unique ID, of sorts).[10]

IPFS and the Maze of Healthcare Records

This data structure is the successor to ADS, the authenticated data structure. The initial advantage of ADS was the construction of a data structure whose operations could be carried out by an untrusted prover. Understanding the historical value of ADS makes the benefits of IPFS easier to understand.

Why does this matter? Every patient could create a list of his or her medical records from any provider, all with an address—similar to bookmarking URLs in your favorite Internet browser (only securely).

Medical records are addressable with permanent addresses (medical records with a permanent home).

Versioning of Your Medical Records

The fundamental principle of IPFS is that all data is part of the same Merkle-DAG, a content-addressed block storage model with content-addressed hyperlinks. It doesn't matter where your information is located. As long as the address structure is standardized, this information could be accessible from any platform, database, or system.

Unlike traditional, networked, provider-to-provider systems, with IPFS, there are no privileged nodes. IPFS is the result of a mashing of distributed hash tables (DHT), BitTorrent, Git, and Self-Certified Filesystems. The IPFS protocol also contains a set of eight subprotocols or principles that synthesize prior peer-to-peer concepts that assemble to form the backbone of IPFS:

1. **Identities:** peer node identification.
2. **Network:** govern the connections to other peers.
3. **Routing:** information relevant to locate peers and stored objects.
4. **Exchange:** protocol managing how blocks are distributed.
5. **Objects:** Merkle-DAG, content-addressable immutable objects, and links.
6. **Files:** a versioned, controlled file system.
7. **Naming:** mutable naming (permanent objects) with content-addressed DAG objects.
8. **Applications:** any application that's running over IPFS to leverage the new connected web.

The IPFS stack is a combination of eight elements: identity (of each node) + network + routing (distributed hash tables) + exchange (BitTorrent) + Merkle-Dag (Git) + naming (Self-Certified Filesystems) + applications (web). Together, these elements form the IPFS stack—a stack that will be used to standardize the accessibility of medical records.

IPFS is the most impactful data structure you haven't yet discovered. Building a new application? You should consider IPFS compatibility. Establishing an innovative, data-centric value offering? If you're not discussing IPFS, you're heading in the wrong direction.

The Merkle Tree for Connected Health

Be prepared for the blockchain discussion by improving your knowledge of Merkle trees and Merkle-DAGs. Do you know how they relate to healthcare?

It's the application of technology, not the technology itself, that provides for business transformation. Making the connection between how the technology works and how it applies to healthcare can be perplexing. Let's untie the knot of Merkle trees and Merkle-DAGs and connect these innovations to healthcare.

A MERKLE TREE

Hash values are numeric values created from data. Hash values uniquely identify data and provide a "digital fingerprint." These values are used to validate that data hasn't been tampered with or altered.

The Merkle tree was named after Ralph Merkle, one of the inventors of public key encryption and a researcher on cryonics (suspension and storage services of humans). In 1979, Merkle wrote a paper titled, "Secrecy, Authentication and Public Key Systems," in which he presented his thesis findings on cryptography.[11]

The Merkle tree is a cascading network of hashes (or hash trees). This binary tree structure is used to condense transactions that are hashed into a block.

The Merkle tree structure is important because it allows miners to verify the hashes of blocks. Think of a tree with all the minor branches connected into larger branches, which eventually connect to the trunk of the tree or the "root hash."

For example, let's assume you have a single block and you want to verify the authenticity of that block. You'll first need the root hash (a collection of block hashes) and the blocks in the transaction tree (or series) that, together, will allow the reconstruction of the hash tree for blocks you didn't generate.

Objects in a typical Merkle tree are linked together by the blocks' transaction sequence. Therefore, you need all or some of that transaction history (collection of hashes) to confirm authenticity. At some point, scale becomes a challenge or, at minimum, a point of discussion.

A MERKLE-DAG

A Merkle-DAG is similar to a Merkle tree in that each is essentially a tree of hashes. A Merkle tree connects transactions by sequence, but a Merkle-DAG connects transactions by hashes. In a Merkle-DAG, addresses are represented by a Merkle hash. This spiderweb of Merkle hashes links data addresses together by a Merkle graph. The directed, acyclic graph (DAG) is used to model information—in our case, modeling what address has stored specific data.

It's useful to know that different blockchains (Ethereum, Bitcoin, Lisk, MultiChain, and Eris) use a variety of implementations of Merkle trees or similar structures.

The Healthcare Connection

Let's put it all together: Merkle trees are used to verify something.

Simply stated, Merkle tree data structures provide state verifications for data. The knowledge of the state also becomes useful when we're talking about healthcare. For example, we can answer queries such as, "Tell me the last time you had a physical?" or "Did you have a blood test done during your last appointment?" We just become much smarter.

By keeping the states in a Merkle-DAG (or hash chain) nodes can verify the validity and correctness of states. The verified state can also be used for searching. It isn't possible for nodes to lie or change a past state. Therefore, nodes cannot change or falsify content. This results in nodes not having to trust each other.

Another interesting beast is the Merkle computer, in which state changes are hash-linked sequentially (think serial log). Merkle trees are used to verify the state.

Allow me to provide an example. Let's assume we have three patients: patient A, patient B, and patient C. It's unlikely all health events from patient C will neatly follow all the health events of patient A and patient B. Most likely, health events for all three patients will be in random order.

Merkle-DAG structures can be used to verify the state of hashes. When used in combination with a Merkle computer, we could process through a list of health events to construct a chronological history of the patient—e.g., healthcare events for patient A and then patient B and, lastly, patient C, even if the actual events were out of our desired grouped sequence.

The New Discussion

Do adequately blockchains scale? Will this evolve into existence or fade into extinction? Many issues remain to be solved. We don't have all the answers. We rarely do.

However, I'm sure of one thing: IPFS and blockchain will gain momentum in healthcare. Interest in these areas will continue to grow as leaders better understand the technological impact on the business of healthcare delivery.

Rest assured, you're better prepared for the blockchain discussion with an upgraded understanding of Merkle trees.

Innovative leaders are learning about IPFS: what it is, where it impacts the organization, and how it can be used to create a strategy to leverage emerging foundational technology for competitive advantages. This is the future of healthcare—a connected web of ecosystems where any data, anywhere, at any time, can be linked and then retrieved, given the proper access rights.

Let's create a new revolution together, a revolution of believers. Healthcare can change. It just requires more believers. If you don't believe for yourself that change in healthcare is possible—believe for someone you love.

"Innovation almost always is not successful the first time out. You try something and it doesn't work, and it takes confidence to say we haven't failed yet... ultimately you become commercially successful."

— CLAYTON CHRISTENSEN

PRACTICAL USE CASES

Blockchain opportunities are changing healthcare globally, and innovative leaders see this change.

The exponential growth of blockchain applications can benefit population health, medical records, and patient-generated data.

The first industry to visibility take advantage of blockchain was financial services. Financial services had the courage to believe in the potential of blockchain technologies and grew a three-tier model:

1. Applications and solutions: brokerages, exchanges, soft wallets, hard wallets, investments, merchants, compliance, trading platforms, capital markets, microtransactions, money services, banks, ATMs, payroll and insurance, payments, trade finance
2. Middleware and services: services, software development, general APIs, special APIs, platforms, smart contracts
3. Infrastructure and base protocols: public, special, payment, miners

Healthcare is late to the show but hasn't totally missed it. Blockchain opportunities are changing healthcare globally. Blockchain is finding its place in a new world.

Why Are Use Cases So Scarce?

Are you trying to apply blockchain to healthcare? Having trouble finding concrete use cases? There's a simple explanation for that.

Are you protecting trade secrets or using innovation as a strategic advantage? Nondisclosure agreements (NDAs) are the reason why you're unable to find specific use cases for a named company.

Have you ever had a great idea only to realize someone else created the product, service, or designed the interaction first? I think we've all experienced this at one time or another. A realization, almost comical, happens the more you're engaged in a field. You're unable to talk about the best ideas. Verbal agreements lead to confidentiality agreements that eventually result in nondisclosure agreements.

At some point, you grow your understanding of a topic from information to knowledge to strategy. It's at the strategy level where it gets dangerous. Why? This is the point at which you have the knowledge and ability to execute. Few leaders will reach out to an expert they don't think can deliver or whose ideas can't be realized.

Frequently, leaders championing innovation efforts are frustrated by the lack of specific or contextual examples of innovation. Recently, this frustration has focused on the difficulty of identifying use cases that apply to blockchain in healthcare. It's not all grim; there's an upside. Here are two examples:

1. A builder is building a new custom house; however, he's not able to talk about the design. If you were considering the development of a custom garage for your boat or plane, the good news is the builder's knowledge will transfer.
2. A doctor designs a patient-care program for a particular patient but is unable to discuss the name or specific situation of the patient. However, that doctor's

knowledge and the themes applied will be useful if you're designing a new patient experience.

Almost all knowledge is transferable. Don't get hung up on the specifics—partner with a leader who can be trusted and has a successful industry track record. When industry experts are engaged at the edge of innovation—creating strategies for sustainable competitive advantage—board members will be quick to ensure their IP is protected. The organization won't want those competitive ideas discussed outside a small circle of trusted and contractually bound individuals.

That expert's professional courtesy—to keep secrets secret—will be extended when exploring new models for profitability for your organization.

Population Health Management

Health information exchanges (HIE) and all-payer claim databases (APCD) have become obsolete with blockchain. It doesn't make sense to trust organizations to verify members' trustworthiness when it's not required with blockchain. Eliminating this prehistoric middleman increases data security and removes the cost, time, and resources required to prove that a party is doing what they say they'll do. New models that share medical records are emerging.

In 2007, the government of Estonia joined forces with Guardtime, a leader in cybersecurity, using blockchain's Keyless Signature Infrastructure (KSI) to provide authentication on a massive scale. Their combined challenge was to verify the integrity of data-at-rest on a global scale.

Estonia is among the few (if not the only) digital societies that has 100% of its medical health records online. Spending time and resources verifying members' trustworthiness (e.g., HIE, all-payer claims database, local EMRs—electronic medical records) no longer makes savvy business sense. Blockchain will leapfrog population health by providing trust where none exists for continuous access to patient records by directly linking information to clinical and financial outcomes.

Population health just got smarter.

Healthcare Mobile Communications and Notifications

Many new blockchain startups offer services to collect data from the Web and mobile apps, record information in the blockchain, and slingshot data to other systems by using REST API or HTML form submissions. Already have an existing mobile application? Leveraging REST APIs can extend functionality and provide a "safe" way to amplify your corporate innovation footprint.

In October 2015, Philips Healthcare announced a joint blockchain project. The partnership extends the reach of Philip Healthcare by partnering with a startup that supports over 400 applications such as Google Sheets, Gmail, and Slack and also assisted the Department of Economic and Community Development of Connecticut to survey 200 top technology companies.

The startup can also handle medical, financial, and legal records through its blockchain integration and infrastructure platform.

PGHD Meets Wearables

Patient-generated health data (PGHD) has tremendous potential, but, to date, it hasn't delivered the promised value—mainly because this data never makes it to the patient.

Wearable technologies such as Under Armour HealthBox, Bragi Dash, Hexoskin smart shirt, and OMSignal OMbra have generated industry excitement while playing safely on the fringe of patient transformation. Wearable tech is exciting, hip, and a great conversation starter. Value alignment is found at the intersection of wearable tech and integration of medical records. FHIR APIs needed to connect patients to EMRs won't be mainstream until 2018. The major EHR vendors aren't going to publish a complete service definition for FHIR profiles to share with software companies. Access to data—not technology or patient behavior—is preventing adoption. No data, no insight.

At the World Economic Forum, personal data was declared a new asset class. Healthbank, based in Switzerland, is a global digital health innovator taking a radically transparent approach to health system transactions. Its approach is a new way of sharing data and uses personal data that's secured. A logical next step for Healthbank would be to incorporate blockchain technology. The Healthbank mantra is "my data, my choice, my Healthbank."

Blockchain applications place personal and patient information into the hands of the individual. Doctor visits, sleep patterns, heart rate, glucose level, and Internet of Things (IoT) devices can all be polled and then stored using the Healthbank blockchain. This innovative blockchain company is attending conferences and telling their story in Finland, Barcelona, and Brazil—the world is watching. Also, Noser Health (Germany) and Netcetera (Switzerland) have recently joined Healthbank as partners to mature its global health data transaction platform.

Once patient-generated data is owned by the patient—and this includes data from wearables to physician and clinical visits—a dramatic shift will occur. Trust is difficult to find in today's global economy. The "cloud" is considered safe— well, at least up until the point that your personal information resides there. Blockchain technology can authenticate access to medical information, quickly and securely.

Innovative leaders can see the change. It's happening now; the patient experience is evolving.

Autonomous Monitoring of Ubiquitous Medical Devices

The immutability of blockchain can improve access to medical information. How will care change over the next three to 10 years? Will the definition of treatment change? Today, when we think of preventive medicine, thoughts of face-to-face appointments with doctors rise to the top of our minds. Tomorrow, robotics, nanobots, and nanomachines may be a common part of the new definition of preventive care.

In "The Cryptocitizen Framework for Interoperability with Blockchain," Brandt and I present the concept of blockchain being leveraged for healthcare device maintenance in which nanomachines will autonomously communicate device-to-device:[1]

> Device-to-device distributed sharing will create a new market for semi-autonomous devices. These devices—such as delivery robots providing medical goods throughout a hospital autonomously or disinfection robots that interact with people with known infectious diseases such as healthcare-associated infections (HAIs)—will report information not to a central authority but to other devices. Medical nanotechnology is expected to employ nanorobots that will be injected into the patient to perform work at a cellular level. Ingestibles and internables bring forward the introduction of broadband-enabled, digital tools that are eaten and "smart" pills that use wireless technology to help monitor internal reactions to medications. Medical nanotechnology is just the beginning.[2]

MONITORING ATRIAL FIBRILLATION WITH THE BLOCKCHAIN

Adding color to the research proposition, we offer this example of how medical device maintenance is possible with blockchain:

> The following is an example of how blockchain technologies could manage medical devices. A patient named

John, who has atrial fibrillation, has an atrial defibrillation device implanted: this is commonly known as an Afib device. This implantable defibrillator allows quick restoration of the sinus rhythm by administering a low-energy shock. The Afib device was manufactured by company 'X' with a serial number 'Y.' During manufacturing, a blockchain was created to track this device. The United States Food and Drug Administration (FDA) mandated that a hash of the unique device identifier (UDI) be stored in the blockchain along with other pertinent information. The hash of the device information is stored and verifiable in an immutable digital ledger. The implanted Afib device is assigned to John, and the device's blockchain is updated with information such as the hospital, doctor, emergency contacts, and advance directives around care for John. The Afib device is supported by a series of smart contracts that can autonomously notify John and providers when the device needs service, e.g., battery expiration, or when health irregularities are detected.

Today, device preventive maintenance is rudimentary at best. For example, when an Afib device requires maintenance, the device starts to audibly alarm in the patient's chest, which can be disturbing. A smart contract could also send preventive maintenance information to the patient and provider, reducing the chance of a catastrophic failure.[3]

We present arguments offering new exploratory propositions that require more research. These research propositions identify three areas as requiring more in-depth research relating to blockchain for healthcare:

1. Healthcare device maintenance ranging from medical devices to nanomachines will autonomously communicate device-to-device.
2. Personal and public self-sovereignty will place identity ownership in the hands of the patient.

3. Electronic health information exchanges (HIE) and all-payer claims databases (APCD) will establish trust using blockchain technologies.

Blockchain technologies offer answers to healthcare's interoperability struggle. The solution to this national crisis won't, however, be purely solved by adding yet another layer of technology. The underlying broken payer and provider processes need to be addressed in parallel for a complete, patient-centric solution.

The patient ownership of data accelerates health data transparency. Blockchain technologies can observe what data is being accessed, who can access the data, and for what period. Self-sovereign identity provides sovereignty, security, and privacy to promote benefits for the patient and the organization or agency by reducing risk, strengthening security, improving accuracy, deepening permission control, and decreasing the time required for regulatory oversight.

Teleradiology

Teleradiology is ripe for blockchain. Healthcare image diagnosis and treatment is based on trust; however, it could be based on truth. Let's explore how.

Teleradiology, or remote radiology service, is the future of radiology. Information technology has been the genesis of radiology and nuclear medicine. Nighthawk services have changed the future of work for radiology. All but vascular and interventional radiology is protected from outsourcing. As radiology outsourcing moves to low-wage countries, revisiting the fee-per-report reimbursement scheme is in order. How can the in-house radiologist compete?

Blockchain technology can assist with improving the truth for CT scans, MRIs, and conventional radiographs. Blockchain technology gives radiologists and their patients truth.

Teleradiology for Clinical Applications

Radiology is the science of high-energy radiation for the diagnosis and treatment of disease. Teleradiology extends this definition into the transmission of radiological patient images—X-rays, CT scans, and MRIs, for example.

Diagnostic imaging modalities—used by doctors to diagnose a disease or illness—vary based on clinical need. I'll briefly explain seven of the major types of modalities used today.

1. **Projection (plain) radiography (X-ray):** produced by transmitting X-rays through a patient. Film has been replaced by computed radiography (CR) and, more recently, by digital radiography (DR). Plain radiographs can be used to identify various types of arthritis and pneumonia, bone tumors (especially benign bone tumors), fractures, and congenital skeletal anomalies.

2. **Fluoroscopy and angiography:** generated with a fluorescent screen, an image intensifier tube is connected to a closed-circuit television system. This type of special X-ray image is used to help identify abnormalities such as tumors, cysts, and inflammations.

3. **Computed tomography (CT scan):** CT scans use X-rays combined with computing algorithms to create an image of the body. Often used for urgent or emergent conditions including cerebral hemorrhage, pulmonary embolism (clots in the arteries of the lungs), aortic dissection (tearing of the aortic wall), and obstructing kidney stones.

4. **Ultrasound (echo):** used to visualize soft-tissue structures in the body. Medical ultrasonography uses ultrasound in real time. This imaging technology is useful when observing changes over time—for example, to monitor changes in heart valves and major vessels or in carotid arteries, which may be a warning sign of an impending stroke.

5. **Magnetic resonance imaging (MRI):** uses powerful magnetic fields to align atomic nuclei with body tissues. Among all the imaging modalities, MRI scans give the best soft-tissue contrast. MRIs help doctors to determine if tissues are healthy. They can be used to identify brain tumors, traumatic brain injury, developmental anomalies, multiple sclerosis, stroke, dementia, infection, and the causes of headaches.

6. **Nuclear medicine:** uses radiopharmaceuticals administered into a patient. Positron emission tomography (PET) scans or single-photon emission computed tomography (SPECT) can be used to improve diagnostic accuracy. Nuclear medicine imaging is used to evaluate specific conditions relating to the heart, lungs, thyroid, liver, brain, gallbladder, and bones.

7. **Interventional radiology (IR or VIR):** vascular and interventional radiology are minimally invasive to the patient. Whether for diagnosis (angiography—looking at blood vessels and organs) or treatment (angioplasty—widening obstructed arteries or veins), IR is used to identify disease. Several uses for IR exist, including the diagnosis or treatment of vascular disease, renal artery stenosis, and gastrostomy tube placements.

TELERADIOLOGY'S BUSINESS CASE

Teleradiology is the transmission of radiographic images from one location to another for sharing studies with other radiologists and physicians. The benefits of teleradiology have mirrored the benefits of telehealth. A doctor in New York who needs the results of a scan can transmit that image to the West Coast or overseas to ensure a timely reading.

The primary benefit of blockchain technologies, when applied to teleradiology, is they offer "truth" not "trust." This is accomplished by offering an integrity check on patient images. Yesterday, radiologists had to trust that images were accurate and unaltered—but they had no proof. Today, they have truth—immutable evidence that the images they're reading are unchanged.

Does this add value? You tell me. Let's assume you're a patient. When your doctor made a diagnosis based on an image of your body, would it matter to know, with near 100 percent certainty, that the image was unaltered? It would matter to me. Let's assume you can choose two providers to read your image. The first provider ensures that the image is unaltered. The second provider claims to have high security but offers no guarantees that the image is unaltered. Which provider would you choose?

Truth over trust is what should define the business case for teleradiology—patient image proof for treatment and diagnosis.

As a recent study found, one in 20 (or 12 million) adults in the United States is misdiagnosed annually.[4] Most patients won't gamble on their health when the circumstances are severe enough to warrant a scan.

Immutable Patient Images

We can expand the business case for teleradiology to include image transmission. By using blockchain technology, improved patient image immutability ensures a provider can validate that the image and diagnosis are unchanged. Providers can verify they're reviewing the latest copy and confirm the "right" image version was received.

This proof can be incorporated into the image display view for clinicians. For example, an image would have three statuses for "image validation:"

1. **Confirmed:** A green check mark would appear if the image were validated and unaltered.
2. **Untrusted:** A red "X" indicates the image had been manipulated.

3. **Unknown:** A gray question mark could be used if there was a connectivity problem.

If a clinician was so inclined, he or she could select "image validation" and view the patient image detail, which would include the following:

1. **Visual confirmation:** the "image validation" discussed previously.
2. **Transaction ID:** blockchain address.
3. **Hash:** hash value.
4. **Received:** the date and time presented to the user.
5. **Confirmation:** date and time the transaction was committed.
6. **Visual chart:** illustration of associated linked images.
7. **Local stored:** date and time with an internal reference number.

Together, these attributes present proof the image was unchanged. Using these principles, blockchain technology can create proof of receipt and transmission of Digital Imaging and Communications in Medicine (DICOM) data. DICOM is a standard for the handling, storing, printing, and transmitting of information in medical imaging.

A FEW MYTHS DEBUNKED

Are patient records stored on the blockchain?

No. The blockchain provides a check of the patient image (a hash similar to a checksum function) to ensure the record hasn't been tampered with. The patient image and data don't live on the blockchain.

Is the blockchain able to handle large record sizes?

A common misconception is that patient images will be transferred to a blockchain. This isn't how it works. The patient image is transferred to an existing image repository. Only the check or hash would reside on the blockchain, not the image.

Do blockchain projects in healthcare require significant changes to core technology?

No. The imaging workflow isn't changed. To implement, simply add a new workflow that records the data source in a digital ledger. A basic check can then be used to verify the data source is unchanged.

Doesn't blockchain data need to be encrypted?

Nope. Remember, the patient image isn't stored on a blockchain, only the hash. Unless you hold the private and public key, you're unable to make use of the data.

You'd use the same standard security protocols for transferring data. There's a proposal from the MIT Media Lab to address the protection of personal data.

Is additional infrastructure required to bolt-on blockchain for encryption?

The short answer is no. Often, healthcare leaders who start to research blockchain mistakenly feel data needs to be encrypted. The data that's being transmitted to the blockchain isn't subject to HIPAA regulations; it's not protected health information. Remember, the image isn't being transmitted to the blockchain, only the hash.

MIT has an active project exploring a peer-to-peer network that allows users to share their data with cryptographic privacy guarantees. This would be useful when the patient knows their relative position in the group but learns nothing about other members' "diagnoses." This community-based approach for data analytics could be leveraged to allow patients to conditionally share image diagnoses for the benefit of the crowd.

The Radiological Society of North America (RSNA), the American College of Radiology, and the International Society for Magnetic Resonance in Medicine (ISMRM) have lots of additional information on radiology. For a complete list of domestic and international radiological associations, Radiology.org is a great resource.

THE PATH TO IMPLEMENTATION

Are you thinking about applying blockchain technology for teleradiology? There are many ways to exploit the benefits of blockchain technologies. Blockchain's characteristics of distributed, public, time-stamped, and persistently established proof give providers immutable proof that sensitive data hasn't been altered. When it comes to your health, would you rather have trust or indisputable truth that your patient images haven't been changed?

Blockchain Applications

There are a multitude of blockchain applications, but they all lead back to one cardinal question: How can blockchain technology be monetized for healthcare?

SMART HEALTH CONTRACTS

The global pharmaceutical market is $1.057 trillion, and the major players include Pfizer ($47.4 billion), Johnson & Johnson ($16.3 billion), Humira ($11.84 billion), and Novartis AG ($49.4 billion). The race to anonymously cross reference enormous sets of dynamic medical data with historical medical records will open revenue streams for drug discovery and personalized medicine.

Smart contracts execute the obligations under the agreement to which both parties have agreed. Blockchain offers a reliable environment for these contracts because of the immutability and cryptographic security strength of the blockchain. This may be the next-generation electronic medical record. However, that's just the beginning.

The entire office visit would be executed through a physician visit-distributed application. This application would seamlessly manage admittance, access the patient's universal EMR, and validate the patient's identity and access. Once the patient had completed their doctor appointment, the software would annotate the universal EMR and complete the checkout including processing the patient's payment.

Web services and daemons have no internal capital. Decentralized applications (Dapps) are the simplest form of a smart contract. This is an agreement involving digital assets between two parties that get automatically redistributed based on the contracted formula. Decentralized organizations (DOs) are composed of a set of properties that can be digital and a protocol that defines the rules for a group of individuals. Decentralized autonomous organizations (DAOs) have internal capital that's valuable. Smart contracts may free DAOs from the risky human component by leveraging blockchain architecture, inching DAOs closer to real AI.

In the blockchain model, patient records can't be hacked or stolen. The process for requesting, receiving, and paying for care will be facilitated through authorization (hashes) on the blockchain.

Universal Ledger for Global Genomic Sequencing

Once personal genome sequencing becomes part of the mainstream, 322.7 million Americans will need a secure way to store and access their genomes.

We know that individual genomes vary by less than 1% and can roughly be compressed to 4 megabytes. The human genome contains an estimated 2.9 billion base pairs. However, storage in 2-bit representation is impractical. Also, when working with genomic data, it's stored and researched by chromosome, not in long data streams. Individual chromosome data storage can range from 50MB to 300MB, based on several variables. To keep things simple, let's assume a human genome takes 725 megabytes (2.9 base pairs times 2) to store. There are creative ways to compress this data using

GARLI (performs heuristic, phylogenetic searches).[5] Where is this data going to live and how will it be accessed?

DNA.bits, founded in 2014, is a cutting-edge technology company that solves the challenge of mapping large data sets to clinical data. Using authentication without identification, DNA.bits can correlate large populations of genetic samples focusing on HIPAA, genomics, and de-identified continuous sharing of genetic and correlated clinical data.

DNA.bits utilizes the Bitcoin platform and can aggregate data from multiple sources without the need to collect it into a central database. What value would you assign to this mapping function?

Peer-to-Peer (P2P) Insurance

Dynamis (Virginia, USA), Inspeer (Paris, France), PeerCover (Tasman, New Zealand), Friendsurance (Berlin, Germany), Lemonade (New York, USA), Guevara (United Kingdom), and TongJuBao (China) are applying the crowdfunding platform to insurance. The general concept is to make insurance more affordable. Policyholders pool together for coverage and, when there's a claim, they use that pooled money to pay the claim. If there are no claims, the policy cost will decrease. Microinsurance might unseat large insurance companies.

Zopa was the first to start peer-to-peer lending in 2004. Zopa applied the sharing economy to lending a decade ago; new players are applying the sharing economy to personal insurance. At a macro level, there are two keystone benefits: (1) pooling of shared risk and (2) the pooling of shared benefits.

Economies of scale help suppress out-of-pocket costs for policy holders, and insurance companies benefit because they carry a smaller annual risk profile as a result of paying less outbound for claims incurred by the policy group.

The P2P insurance model also benefits from the lack of trust between providers and members. Blockchain offers trust between strangers. Users interacting with web servers place trust in a root administrator. However, as experienced by Hollywood Presbyterian Medical Center (ransomware), VTech (data breach), and Patreon(data breach), these architectures are susceptible to intrusion.

Web services offer a bit more security when they're architected properly, yet these schemes depend entirely on trusting the computer or the people that have access to the computer.

The blockchain isn't necessarily a "trustless architecture," but it does offer a "trust-minimized" solution. In this situation, subscribers would trust the code and could still not trust the owner of the computer or code.

Peer-to-peer insurance that leverages the blockchain can decrease policyholders' costs while improving the security and trust of the network.

Quantified Self-Data Standards

Biometrics integrated into quantified self-data (e.g., data from your Fitbit) could be integrated into the health blockchain. Blockchain presents many opportunities to improve existing process and business models including decentralized data access, universal EMRs, digital health asset protection, health tokens, and even DNA wallets.

As executives, our challenge is to simplify blockchain's value. Blockchains decentralize businesses and remove the middleman. They establish digital trust in a trustless world, and we need more trust in healthcare.

Trust with Chain-of-Custody

Blockchain consensus and chain-of-custody for the healthcare supply chain are coming to your neighborhood.

User-facing applications, purchase decisions, and infrastructure have never aligned for healthcare. The patient is still waiting, and the experience of care is disjointed. Sure, many of us dreamers have tried to achieve alignment, but, ultimately, the seamless integration of health has yet to be fully discovered. Interoperability, auditability, cost-efficiency, real-time and agile enrollments, public transparency, and guaranteed continuity (removal of the central operator) are what blockchain offers healthcare.

TRUST IN PRODUCT SUPPLY CHAINS

Nike, Coca-Cola, and Apple are brands we trust. What if every corporation had the same opportunity to build confidence in their company and their products? They do with blockchain.

Large transnational corporations are top-of-mind when we think of trust. Turn the spotlight onto healthcare. What comes to mind when you think about your healthcare insurer? Is trust the first thing you imagine when you hear United Health Group, Aetna, Cigna, or Blue Cross? It's unlikely. They also aren't solely to blame for the lack of trust in the healthcare system. Insurers are only a spoke in the broken wheel of healthcare, subject to the same dysfunction as the other healthcare actors.

Healthcare delivery systems are also accountable for the disintegration of the United States healthcare system. Healthcare delivery systems include:

- Hospitals and acute-care facilities
- Healthcare networks
- Ambulatory/outpatient provider practices (individual, group, and clinic)
- Health plans
- Payers (insurers)
- Ancillary service providers (laboratory, radiology)
- Pharmacy/pharmacy benefits managers (PBMs)
- Health information organizations (HIO)
- Health information exchanges (HIE)
- Critical-access or rural hospitals
- Health insurance exchanges (HIX)

- Public sector agencies (public health departments)
- Clearing houses and others

Do you trust the products you consume? What do you know about products you use every day? What was the supply chain of your toothbrush? How about the chain-of-custody of your medical record for the most recent diagnosis? Your appointment could have been to treat the common cold or something more serious.

- Who's seen the diagnosis?
- Does your electronic toothbrush deplete natural resources?
- Are the meat and seafood you're eating contaminated?

Berks Parking recalled 1,320 pounds of beer products in January 2016, and Hormel Foods had a beef recall in February 2016, according to Consumer Affairs. These are the ones we know about. What about future contaminations?

John West, a fish supplier out of the U.K., provides canned tuna and salmon products that allow consumers to track their fish from the boat to the can.[6] This additional standard placed on John West products resulted in $24.2 million worth of increased sales.

Consumers care about the supply chain; the value of transparency is real, and it can be applied to improve your heath.

Medical Record Chain-of-Custody

With a centralized chain-of-custody (CoC), fraud can easily occur. We have to look no further than the timber industry and CoC certification to understand why former Forest Stewardship Council (FSC) General Director André de Freitas recently called the CoC certification a myth. Forest Stewardship Council, Programme for the Endorsement of Forest Certification (PEFC), and agricultural schemes such as Fairtrade and

133

SAN/Rainforest Alliance all evolved while adding risk to their primary mission or eco-labeled products.

Blockchain allows organizations to operate and conduct commerce in a trustless and permissionless ecosystem while allowing the consumer to discover the full supply chain of his or her toothbrush, food products, and even medical records.

Blockchain's Transactional Process for Health

Distributed ledgers, mining, and cryptographic nonce make blockchain confusing and hard to explain. Articulating the value of blockchain becomes even more challenging when applying the technology to healthcare. Welcome to the modern and fashionable EMR.

Allow me to expand: The doctor confirms the diagnosis, the provider confirms treatment was performed, and the payer confirms valid insurance coverage. The peer review is also where consensus occurs. It could be as simple as requiring your doctor and provider to use public keys to create consensus, or agreement could be based on a threshold cryptosystem (mainly for the military prior to 2012; subsequent versions include: RSA, Paillier cryptosystem, Damgård–Jurik cryptosystem, ElGamal) or ring signatures (a message signed with a ring signature is endorsed by someone in a particular group of people e.g., your family doctor's health practice) or even other cryptographic techniques that could be implemented.

The next explanatory steps update an EMR from the perspective of the blockchain, illuminating the roles among the patient, doctor payer (insurer), and the provider.

1. **Receive token**—a healthcare transaction is received by the blockchain as a set of actions grouped in the form of tokens.
2. **Pull base block**—an historical block will be pulled (the last block confirmed) including an identifier for the block that's used to create the new block.

3. **Peer review**—the token is validated (the set of health-care actions, enrollment information, proof-of-insurance, diagnosis, and procedure codes for treatment) and broadcasted to named peers for review.

4. **Validation of block**—at this point, the digital signature of the validators is added to the block (hashed).

5. **Token extended**—the initial health token (the set of actions) is extended to include the validity token from the confirm health actions

6. **Block creation**—based on the validity token, historical block identifier, digital signatures, peer reviews, and the set of healthcare tokens. Then miners calculate and generate the new block.

7. **Block broadcast**—using the blockchain, Health Record Bank (bcHRB), and the peer-reviewed token(s), these combined blocks (sets of healthcare actions) are then broadcast to peers.

Note: Nik Custodio did a great job explaining, at a high level, how this process works on Medium, if there's any confusion.[7]

To summarize, a token is received containing healthcare transactions (medical, dental, pharmacy, or ancillary services) and a historical block identifier is used as the start of the base new block. The token—a set of healthcare transactions—is peer reviewed and validated once the peer review is completed. Digital signatures are added to the block, extending the token.

Once the healthcare token, historical identifiers (previous block), peer-reviewed validated token, and digital signatures are complete, the miners create a new block reflecting the recently received healthcare transactions. Miners then broadcast to peers on the bcHRB.

Instead of medical data sitting across silos with limited interoperability, with blockchain, we now have the ability to move the information in a secure, auditable, and shared data layer. Transparency isn't only about the supply of goods; it also involves services—healthcare services.

The Music of Blockchain

Blockchain smart contracts provide the bridge connecting the shared experience of the music and health industries.

Music shapes culture, entertainment, and technology. The passion for music spans industries, refreshes ideas, and introduces new concepts previously invisible. The music industry's maturation into digital contexts and its exploration of blockchain technology have uncovered lessons we can apply to healthcare.

INTERSECTING MUSIC AND HEALTH

The world is growing, and the music industry is shrinking. Economies of scale exist yet, each year, these miss the opportunity to impact healthcare for the better. The music and healthcare industries are managing the transition from the physical to digital. How will the music industry keep pace with the trends of instant access and play anywhere? How will the healthcare industry keep pace with the trends of instant access and viewing medical information anywhere? The blockchain is the answer. Smart contracts provide the bridge.

MUSICAL REVENUE FRAGMENTATION

The music industry is getting a shakeup but continues to lose out in revenue. The end of 2014 marked the first year that the industry derived the same revenue from digital channels (46 percent) as from physical format sales (46 percent). According to the United Nation's Department of Economic and Social Affairs Population Division, there are 7.4 billion people in the world today, and the global population is growing by roughly 80 million a year. It's discouraging to realize that the global recorded music industry was a $40-billion business in 1997, but, in 2014, the music industry's global digital revenues barely reached $6.85 billion, according to the International Federation of the Phonographic Industry (IFPI). The IFPI represents the recording industry worldwide and has more than 1,300 record companies in over 57 countries as members.

More people are listening to music, and fewer songwriters and artists are getting paid for their work. Society needs a music industry that rewards people for creating great content, not a scene where music companies wrestle over ownership rights.

HITTING THE MUSIC INDUSTRY WITH PEER-TO-PEER
The introduction of the Bitcoin peer-to-peer electronic cash system by Satoshi Nakamoto (pseudonym) in 2008 immediately sparked the interest of the music industry. The wonder started with companies like Murfie, a music marketplace founded in 2011 that accepts bitcoins as payment for music downloads. Bitcoin, as a payment method, isn't going to change musicians' lives by becoming a new financial standard for payment. However, the application of the blockchain technology to the music industry may change artists' lives.

Blockchain has the potential to modernize every industry in the world. We just don't know exactly how.

It was common knowledge that blockchain could impact the music industry, but the full impact on the industry wasn't articulated clearly to encapsulate the potential for positive change until last month. Benji Rogers published an interesting article on Medium that offers a powerful argument in support of the positive impact that blockchain technology (Ethereum, Muse, Rootstock) would have on the entertainment industry.[8] Later, in part two of his post, Rogers published an update that provided substantive support—both theoretical and technical—on how this could be accomplished, highlighting four clear points:

1. Smart contracts will be the enabler.
2. Blockchain will house a Fair Trade Global Database of rights.

3. Every song will contain Fair Trade Minimum Viable Data (MVD).
4. The new format will be called .bc or "dot Blockchain," a non-replicable wrapper (.bc compliant systems).
5. Music ownership obfuscation will be eliminated.

Will the music industry see the beauty in the blockchain scheme? Blockchain technology applied to your music means that everyone will pay for its use, driving transparency of music ownership. The artist would create a .bc file containing who owns the work and who to pay when used. The music enthusiast, using a platform (YouTube, Spotify, SoundCloud, 8Tracks, Tidal, Pandora, Apple), buys and pays for music as they do today. The difference is that, behind the scenes, a digital ledger tracks ownership of the author and usage rights of the music enthusiast.

Rogers suggests the artist(s) and the music rights' holder(s) define the rules governing play at the time of encoding as part of the song's Fair Trade Minimum Viable Data. The author, composers, contributors, owners, and usage rights are defined as part of smart contracts enabled by blockchain technologies. The music enthusiast also benefits by paying only for what he or she plays via instant payment, and the content is multi-platform accessible. The .bc was envisioned to replace DVD and Blu-Ray and support a new virtual reality (VR) format that has no standardized format or wrapper. This format would contain Minimal Viable Data using the W3C Web standard JSON-LD, illustrated in the dot blockchain concept illustration.[9]

The music industry has struggled with digital rights management (DRM) for years. Blockchain provides a ledger as a means of payment, an automatic royalty payment splitter, and simplified licensing using legal, enforceable, non-ambiguous smart contracts. This concept is more than DRM. It is DRM+.

MUSIC REENERGIZING HEALTH

Blockchain technology can improve transparency of ownership for music as well as health records. The music industry's song ownership challenge parallels the healthcare industry's problem with medical health record ownership. The U.S. insurance industry's net premiums written totaled $1.2 trillion in 2015.[10]

How much more transparency in your personal medical records have you seen in 2016 compared to 2017? I'll share my experience between 2016 and 2017; I saw zero positive impact toward better visibly of my medical records. Personal health records continue to be fragmented among providers and physicians, just as song ownership and royalty payments are scattered throughout the music industry.

Platform scale, interoperability, and privacy are surmountable challenges. How do we transfer trust when patients have no faith in the system? Payments don't reflect treatment provided. We can't blame patients for their lack of confidence when even experts have trouble explaining the circus we call today's "healthcare system."

Blockchain has the potential to give patients, like you and I, hope and restore trust in healthcare. Transparency and ownership of our medical records are the beginning. New healthcare platforms will emerge, returning medical record ownership to the patient.

The New State of Healthcare: State Channels

State channels, ring signatures or confidential signatures, and zero-knowledge proofs (ZKPs) will quickly be common watercooler talk as their impacts on healthcare are made more apparent.

Innovative CIOs will be among the first to link state channels to better health outcomes—running blockchain technologies within their operations.

Blockchain technology scalability challenges are mentioned in virtually every article, video, and podcast on the topic created within the past twelve months. The reality is that the problem of scalability of blockchain technologies has already been technically solved with multiple viable options.

Previously, we covered interactive and zero-knowledge proofs for better patient interactions with blockchain technology. We also discussed zero-knowledge proofs and their impact on healthcare.

State Channels and Dapps

Now we'll cover state channels and ring signatures or confidential signatures and their potential for healthcare when leveraging blockchain technologies. As you read, start to think about the decentralized application (Dapp) for mobile and the tremendous use cases for healthcare.

QUICK DEFINITIONS

Before we begin, it's helpful to get some simple definitions out of the way that are necessary to frame our discussion.

- **Zero-knowledge proofs:** a protocol between two parties in which one party, called the prover, tries to prove an absolute fact to the other party, called the verifier. This concept is used for identification and authentication.
- **State-channels:** Similar to a lightning network payment channel, the state or condition is updated between participants but isn't published on the blockchain.
- **Ring signatures or confidential signatures:** a crypto method to preserve the privacy of the attributes of a person relying on a smart contract.

THE SPARKLE OF STATE CHANNELS

State channels go back to the days of wireless communication.[11] Recently, state channels on Bitcoin were pure payment channels for two parties to send fee-less micropayments.[12] However, lately, they've been used to rethink interactions on the blockchain and, more specifically, off the blockchain.

Why keep information (meaning, the hashes) off the blockchain? Two primary reasons: cost and speed. In general, states are simply interactions between two parties that can apply to any smart contract.

State channels update business processes or transaction states. There's often confusion between state and status; I'll attempt to clarify these terms. While they're similar, they're distinctly different and aren't interchangeable. The state is a condition, e.g., no implicit ordering or position among the states. Status is a rank, e.g., within a process list.

State channels are comprised of three basic properties:

1. **Locking:** the on-chain transaction is locked with a smart contract, and participants must agree to smart contract terms using one of various authentication methods.
2. **Interacting off-chain:** transactions off-chain are linear, just like in the chain. The latest interaction overlays previous transactions. However, only the last state or activity makes its way to the blockchain.
3. **Publishing:** once the operation is complete, the state channel closes and unlocks the smart contract using the most recent update as the primary transaction (this becomes important if Internet connection is lost; at least one node must be online with the latest transaction copy).

This process works well with micropayments and also can be applied to healthcare transactions.

Healthcare's Need for State Channels

Blockchain technologies can solve one of the biggest challenges in healthcare: trust.

Have you been to the doctor recently? Did you know whether the doctor was looking at your most recent medical information or an old copy? Did you bother to ask or verify that he or she was making medical decisions based on the best information—information you validated as the most accurate and up-to-date? This is where blockchain technologies come into play.

They're not going to solve problems related to poor data quality or clumsy data entry, but blockchain technologies, when applied to healthcare, can give us back the trust we've lost in our system of care. As health events are written to the blockchain and the volume of events increases, scalability becomes a challenge. According to a paper by Poon and Dryja entitled, "The BitCoin Lightning Network: Scalable Off-Chain Instant Payments," the Bitcoin lightning network inspired much of the discussion of state channels forming off-chain networks: a network of channels.[13] For our purposes, the exact implementation is less important, but it's available in their paper if you're curious.

The principle presented in this paper states that lightning achieves Bitcoin scalability using an extensive network of micropayment channels. ""If we presume a large network of channels on the Bitcoin blockchain, and all Bitcoin users are participating on this graph by having at least one channel open on the Bitcoin blockchain, it's possible to create a near-infinite amount of transactions inside this network."[14]

What if we apply this to a healthcare ecosystem—a network of payers and providers working in collaboration for the benefit of patients? The healthcare ecosystem becomes a global network that could support near-infinite health events. Picture that for a minute: A global network for healthcare impacting virtually every life in the world. Every life. Now, we narrow the focus to practical solutions for state channels, whether leveraging state channels, sidechains, or the like. Let's ideate on two potential applications for healthcare.

Post-EHR data validation updates: many providers are frustrated by the frequent, significant software updates required for secure and functional EHR technology. How is the state of medical data verified post-upgrade? It's not. State channels offer a method to ensure cryptographic proof of data while not bogging down the blockchain.

Patient admittance and discharge: many patients spend their entire episode of care at a single facility—not over their lifetime but per health event. Why would we update the blockchain at every activity performed for that patient during their stay? We could use a state channel to capture that episode of care, opening the smart contract on admission, and update the state (and health events) within the state channel, off the blockchain.

Once the patient is discharged, the state channel closes and the smart contract publishes what the patient has conditionally authorized to hit the blockchain (the hash of the collective health events). This process avoids the scalability problem and ensures that iterations of the states aren't posted in excess to the blockchain.

ADOPTION IS A DECISION

Make your decision early; your customers will thank you.

The term "Cloud" was first used in 1977 to represent computing networks in ARPANET—pre-Internet, almost 40 years ago. It wasn't until 2009 that the low cost of storage, high-capacity networks, cheap computing power, and the adoption of hardware virtualization, service-oriented architecture, and autonomic and utility computing led to growth in cloud computing. When did your company truly buy into cloud computing? Do you wish you'd adopted earlier?

Achieving scale takes time. Make the decision today to start experimenting with blockchain technologies. Blockchain's potential to improve healthcare may surprise you.

ZKP: The New Intake Experience

Zero-knowledge proofs, when combined with blockchain technologies running on smart contracts, have the potential to prove patient health information without the verifier ever learning anything except that a statement is true.

Imagine for a minute all the healthcare situations where proof is required. Proof of a patient's healthcare coverage. Proof of a patient's name. Proof of a patient's medical history. Proof of a patient's prescription. Each question could be answered without the verifier (hospital receptionist, doctor, or pharmacist) knowing anything except that the statement you told them was true. This is the power of zero-knowledge proofs.

IDEATION OF ZERO-KNOWLEDGE PROOFS

In 1985, three researchers — Shafi (MIT), Micali (MIT), and Rackoff (University of Toronto)—drafted a paper titled, "The Knowledge Complexity of Interactive Proof-Systems."[15] Their research introduced, first, a theorem-proving procedure—a new, efficient method of communicating a proof. The second part of the paper addressed the following question: How much knowledge should be communicated for proving a theorem, T?

We're attempting to convince a verifier of the truth. The idea behind zero-knowledge proofs is that the verifier doesn't learn anything except that a statement is true. What exactly is meant by "doesn't learn anything?" Questions must be answered to formally define the zero-knowledgeness property. The specifics of zero-knowledgeness properties have been explained in a good summary paper.[16] Also, due to the math required to explain the concepts of the zero-knowledgeness properties adequately, I won't be covering that here. We'll focus on the broader applications for healthcare.

For now, you'll have to take my word for it: The math plays out.

PRINCIPLES OF ZERO-KNOWLEDGE PROOFS

Zero-knowledge proofs have three important properties: completeness, soundness, and zero-knowledge.

1. **Completeness:** The verifier always accepts the proof if the fact is true and both parties follow the protocol.
2. **Soundness:** The verifier always rejects the proof if the fact is false as long as the verifier follows the protocol.
3. **Zero-knowledge:** The verifier learns nothing else about the fact being proved from the prover that couldn't be learned without the prover, regardless of following the protocol. The verifier cannot even prove the fact to anyone later.

By leveraging blockchain technologies and smart contracts, we can ensure both parties follow the protocol.

APPLYING ZERO-KNOWLEDGE PROOFS TO HEALTHCARE

Let's apply this to healthcare. As you recall, the initial question presented by Shafi, Micali, and Rackoff (collectively referred to as SMR) was, How much knowledge should be communicated for proving a theorem, T? We can restate this question to be patient-centric and healthcare-specific:

1. How much information does a hospital receptionist require about a patient to check the patient into the facility (hospital, provider, or other)?
2. What are the minimum pieces of information required to be shared with a hospital receptionist to demonstrate a patient's proof of valid health insurance?
3. Is it possible to share no personal patient information (think name, DOB, driver's license) and still have a pharmacist confirm the patient is able to pick up the prescription with the assurance it's the drug ordered?

As mentioned earlier, an interactive and zero-knowledge proof is a protocol between two parties in which one party, called the prover, tries to prove a particular fact to the other party, called the verifier. This concept is used for identification and authentication. Let's look at our three questions again, now considering the role of the verifier and prover.

1. How much information does a hospital (verifier) receptionist require about a patient (prover) to check the patient into the facility (hospital, provider, or other)?
2. What are the minimum pieces of information required to be shared with a hospital receptionist (verifier) to demonstrate a patient's (prover) proof of valid health insurance?
3. Is it possible to share no personal patient information (think name, DOB, driver's license) and still have a pharmacist (verifier) confirm the patient is able to pick up the prescription with the assurance it's the drug ordered for patient (prover)?

ZERO-KNOWLEDGE PROOFS IN PRACTICE

Most zero-knowledge proofs are based on a conversation between the prover and the verifier. This conversation occurs in a series of simulations or interactions that typically progress over a number of iterations:

1. Commitment message from the prover.
2. Challenge from the verifier.
3. Response to the challenge from the prover.

Often, this protocol repeats for several rounds, and then the verifier eventually decides whether to accept or reject the proof based on the prover's responses in all the rounds.

The proof can also be performed efficiently by a simulator that has no idea of what the proof is.

THE VISION

A patient with an Android phone or an iPhone could use a decentralized application (Dapp) to validate patient information during a healthcare event.

Dapps are the simplest form of a smart contract. In our case, this contract could release information to the verifier based on our zero-knowledge-proof smart contract. At the end of the transaction, the verifier would agree that the statement was true—for example, the patient does have medical coverage required for a visit—but without conveying any information apart from the fact that the statement is indeed true.

Proving that one has knowledge of certain information is trivial if one is allowed to reveal that information directly. Knowledge without knowledge—that's the next generation of patient interactions.

"To acquire knowledge, one must study; but to acquire wisdom, one must observe."

— MARILYN VOS SAVANT

CHAPTER 9

HACKING HEALTH & COMPANIES TO WATCH

R edesigning the patient experience requires creative thinking. Remove your constraints and open your mind as we
explore the best commercially viable innovations presented at #YaleHackHealth.

The Yale Healthcare Hackathon was presented by the Yale
Center for Biomedical Innovation and Technology (CBIT)
and the Yale School of Medicine Department of Radiology
and Biomedical Imaging. Over 200 innovators participated
in the hackathon, held January 20 to 22 at the Yale School of
Medicine. Ideas ranged from conceptual—five or more years
out—to innovations based on virtual reality, which, surprisingly, is already here.

In April 2016, the first virtual reality surgery was performed by Dr. Shafi Ahmed, a British physician. The the operation was live-streamed for those without a headset. Those
with a headset were able to download VRinOR and experience the surgery in 360 degrees and real time as Ahmed removed cancerous tissues.

Participants attending the Yale Hackathon were also lucky
to experience live demos of the Microsoft HoloLens, spon-
sored by Photon Biomedical, co-founded by Dr. Daniel Wass-
er and Scott Riddle and based in Philadelphia.

Sometimes, ideas forecast ten years out are practical approaches only years or even months away from entering the
mainstream. Everything of value begins with an idea—even
ideas that initially appear impossible.

Hackathon pitches ranged from wild ideas to grounded,
practical solutions. The final pitches were presented Sunday,

and the presentations were surprisingly practical. Three presentations stood out for creativity, practicability, and commercial viability:

1. RadBit (for patient image portability)
2. Rx4All (a recycling medication program)
3. PAT (a pediatric assistive toy)

Allow me to elaborate on these ideas that seek to re-engineer the patient experience and explore why each one is both unique and practical.

1. RADBIT (PATIENT IMAGE PORTABILITY)

The problem the team solved was improving the portability of medical images that often are degraded during transfer, or the transfer process fails when transferred.

Everyone in the country is a patient, and many of us have had scans (MRIs or CT scans). However, where are those images stored today? CDs containing medical images are often lost. Even when patients do have their CDs, the image files frequently don't work.

RadBit presented an alternative "patient-generated/patient owned" image portability solution. The team built a secure, portable, and permanent image portability solution that leveraged blockchain technology (permissioned digital ledger). The submission included a prototype that was running on a blockchain, showing actual hashes (unique IDs) of several medical images to prove image authenticity. Real functioning code was generated during the hackathon and included in the final presentation along with a video illustrating the workflow for both patients and providers. Using this approach, patients would never lose access to their medical images, and chain of custody would be preserved. The solution offered three core functionalities to enhance medical image portability and immutability: upload, storage, and retrieval.

CNN, Forbes, the Wall Street Journal, the Harvard Business Review, and the Economist are talking about blockchain, and investors are paying attention to blockchain. RadBit extended the economic value of blockchain to healthcare, constructing a portable medical image solution.

RadBit uses a permissioned distributed digital ledger (blockchain) to store images in chronological order. The benefit of blockchain technology, for RadBits, is the creation of a decentralized digital public record of transactions (images) that are secure, anonymous, tamper-proof and unchangeable—a shared single source of truth.

How is blockchain different from a database? The data stored in a blockchain can't be changed or altered. Blockchain uses cryptographic proof (mathematical verification) to confirm no changes have occurred. This concept is similar to a distributed append-only database. Traditional market offerings (like Hugo) don't offer this capability and, therefore, are inherently unsecured. With this solution, clinicians can see proof of image authenticity—a process that today doesn't exist. The creativity of the RadBits solution improves patients' lives with a straightforward and practical approach to medical image retention.

I (representing Quinnipiac University) was fortunate to be a team member of RadBit, along with Brandon Burr (Old Dominion University), Eric Park (Boston University), and Sara Katrancha and Belinda Wu (Yale).

2. RX4ALL (RECYCLING MEDICATION PROGRAM)

The problem this team solved was twofold: Many patients don't have access to medications because they can't afford them, and drugs often expire at healthcare-provider facilities, resulting in wasted medication.

Rx4All, a program for recycling medications, redistributes providers' drugs nearing expiration instead of allowing these expensive drugs to go to waste.

Nonadherence (taking medications are prescribed) is a huge issue and not just for patients. HealthPrize Technologies released a report estimating that global revenue loss as a result of nonadherence has increased from $564 billion in 2012 to $637 billion in 2015. Medical nonadherence accounted for U.S.-based revenue loss of $188 billion in 2012 to $250 billion in 2015. Maybe, if patients received a free trial of a particular medication, they'd see the value in it and continue taking i, often preventing more serious visits to their healthcare providers. Rarely are prescriptions written that are optional. Doctors write prescriptions to effect care outcomes.

The Associated Press has reported that more than 250 million pounds of pharmaceutical waste is generated annually by U.S. hospitals and long-term care facilities, at a cost of $2 billion annually. Harvard Health echoed CDC reports that 8 percent of adult Americans don't take medicines because of the expense, and 75% of these non-compliers (6 percent of all American adults) have private insurance and still don't fill scripts to save money. Nonadherence is significant when combined with the 10 percent on Medicaid and 14 percent with no insurance who are also not filling prescriptions because of the expense. The standard patient strategy is to ask doctors for lower-cost medications, but even lower-cost drugs are sometimes not cheap enough to be affordable.

Rx4All was envisioned as a nonprofit organization seeking to redistribute unopened and unexpired medications to patients in lower socioeconomic classes. The team developed a four-pronged approach:

1. Target nursing homes and hospitals with excess supply of medication.
2. Leverage reverse supply chains with existing distribution channels.
3. Conduct free clinics.
4. Assist patients in the dissemination of near-expiration drugs to decrease disposal costs for providers.

Rx4All was an insightful business model with practical uses targeting seasonal prescription drugs, addressing stock rotation, reducing shelf-life challenges, and utilizing generic launches to promote distribution.

The Rx4All team was made up of Arshad Karin (Infosys), Vanesaa Martinez (UMass Amherst), Pranjal Misra (Infosys), Gina Castillo Piedra (Vassar College) and Joe Voves (R4 Technologies).

3. PAT (PEDIATRIC ASSISTIVE TOY)

The problem this team solved was making hospitals and providers less scary for children.

The team began their presentation describing Ana, a six-year old girl with a special heart who wasn't feeling very good. She was scared, and her parents told her she needed to go to the hospital. Ana's journey began with her feeling bored and lonely waiting in between tests and surgeries. During the span of four days, Ana had to wait for more than 28 hours for her procedure. During this time, more than 35 caregivers touched Ana's case. Scared and in pain, Ana had more than nine tests and one surgery in four days. In Ana's words, "there were so many strangers around me." Companies that are trying to address the problem of making hospitals less scary include Sproutel and Philips, which offers the Philips Ambient experience (a multi-sensorial experience for patients and staff). As Frederick Douglass said, "it is easier to build strong children than to repair broken men."

These methods fall short of the need. They're restricted to a single room, lack trust-building, only temporarily distract patients, and don't provide two-way interactions between the patient and caregivers.

The PAT team's vision was to help Ana feel safe, excited, and empowered throughout her journey. The team's pediatric assistive toy was an interactive system that ran on a wireless device embedded in a friendly toy. It was an empathetic "buddy" designed to entertain, persuade, and educate a child throughout her hospital experience. Picture a talking stuffed frog or monkey that has an interactive iPad-like embedded device that also responds to voice commands. This is a useful and fabulously helpful invention for improving children's comfort during the care experience.

The PAT approach includes caregivers providing input and the involvement of children and family. This friendly toy encapsulates the care experience, providing immediate, non-intimidating patient feedback that can improve restlessness, sleep, pain, and outcomes. PAT is the first interactive patient toy to accompany sick kids at hospitals and at home.

The PAT team was made up of Marina Aldarondo (Rhode Island School of Design), Louis Atallah (Imperial College London), Farzanah Ausaluth (Brown University), Dasha Ivenitsky and Do Hyeon Kevin Park (Vassar College), Alina Khromykh (Harvard University), and Joshua Rafael Segovia (Binghamton University).

Where have you generated your best ideas? When do your best ideas surface? After attending the amazing event hosted by Yale, it's apparent that we can begin to transform healthcare—and it only takes a weekend.

Companies on the Move

Competitors are no longer recognizable. New strategies are required. The game has changed. Today's rules might not apply tomorrow. Learn from blockchain-based healthcare companies that are redefining the rules.

Game theory is the science of strategy—a branch of mathematics and economics that explores strategic situations across multiple stakeholders with different goals, whose actions can affect one another. Pioneering companies are changing the game with blockchain technologies. The new game of consumer interactions redefines transparency, immutability, and security across industries.

NEW GAME WITH NEW PLAYERS

Much progress has been made with game theory. John von Neumann and Oskar Morgenstern's 1944 book, *Game Theory and Economic Behavior*, outlined classic game theory.[1] Franklin D. Roosevelt stated that "competition has been shown to be useful up to a certain point and no further, but cooperation, which is the thing we must strive for today, begins where competition leaves off."

Game theory analyzes strategic interaction and can be applied to economics, political science, and military science. In game theory, players (decision-makers) adopt strategies (complete plans of action), and receive payoffs (rewards or punishments), all of which depend on the strategies of all of the players. A strategy is a complete plan that describes the action a player will take in every circumstance that's observed.

There are many common examples of game theory including elections, auctions, wars, the arms race, oligopolies (when a small number of companies dominate a market), certain aspects of animal behavior, the evolution of social norms, and, of course, games such as the ones played for entertainment, like Pokémon GO.

If you've played the board games Monopoly, Risk, or Stratego, you knew who you were playing the game against. Today, players are less obvious. Likewise, partners you wouldn't consider yesterday might be your best avenue for a competitive advantage. Le'ts explore changing the rules with three of the leaders in blockchain technology.

1. BRON.TECH (SYDNEY, AUSTRALIA)

Problem: Proving identity requires sharing too much identifiable information.

Why play today's game with yesterday's identity solutions? Bron.tech is revolutionizing identity through the bold vision of a personally controlled, digital identity platform to encompass the legal, social, and psychological aspect of one's identity. Bron.tech has three flagship interaction offerings.

OWLEE is a distributed application (Dapp) reputation system providing instantaneous verification, identity management, and interoperability for education providers, organizations, and professionals.

Using blockchain Digital ID, Bron.tech's ID platform is the solution for issuance, verification, and use of digital identities by leveraging cryptography and storing transaction proofs on a public or private immutable ledger (blockchain). It uses multiparty computation enabled by the blockchain to share an identity.

Cyph.MD is a healthcare data-sharing platform. It leverages asymmetric cryptography with a hierarchical certificate system whereby every healthcare provider can issue identity tokens to its practitioners to securely communicate and share data across the entire healthcare network.

2. GEM (CALIFORNIA, UNITED STATES)

> Problem: Personalized care is compromised without the privacy and security of the universal infrastructure.

Concerned about the hidden cost of trust over truth? Gem fuels automation with integrity and helps to create data, identity, and logic frameworks that allow companies to share data with industries by customizing participation within a blockchain network. Cross-industry applications are connecting customers to products, services, and interactions. Gem offers three integrity solutions:

- Distributed Resource Registries to define resources managed within a blockchain.
- Multiparty Identity and Access Management to control access to provisioned resources for key management, e.g. manufacturing or IoT and healthcare medical records.

- Logic Automation using rules to streamline data interactions across companies.

3. IBM BLOCKCHAIN ON BLUEMIX (NEW YORK, UNITED STATES)

Problem: People don't own their data.

Attempting to secure digital assets? IBM Blockchain on Bluemix digitizes transaction workflow and secures digital assets within a private, virtualized environment. IBM Blockchain allows companies to manage, develop, and test blockchain network technology using flexible platforms and infrastructure offerings. These core principles make up the IBM blockchain approach: community (over 44,000 lines of code donated to the Hyperledger Project), cloud (value-based services such as high-availability, compliance, and security) and client (capabilities with the building, piloting, and implementing).

IBM Blockchain on Bluemix enables enterprise blockchain solutions at scale.

Hyperledger Project facilitates open-source, openly governed, cross-industry-enabled blockchain technology.

Docker Hub is designed to help companies deploy and support distributed applications throughout the entire life cycle.

Who's Playing the Game?

The application of game theory in business centers on the interactions of multiple players. Everyone understands games. Competitive pricing to labor negotiations provides similar structures to analyze possible strategies and recommend an optimal strategy for each player. Adam Brandenburger and Barry Nalebuff explained in a Harvard Business Review article how game theory shapes strategy.[2] Whether a high-stakes game or no stakes at all, every game has five elements:

- **Players:** who's involved
- **Added values:** unique value of each player
- **Rules:** structure
- **Tactics:** how players move to shape how other players move
- **Scope:** game boundaries

As you design your organizational innovation strategy and shuffle priorities to determine a place for blockchain, pause to reflect on the game your company is playing and the players at the table. Tthe game might have changed, and you might not notice all the players. Explore partnerships to redefine the rules and create a new game. Be the player in the game that others don't notice.

"The greatest danger in times of turbulence is not the turbulence – it is to act with yesterday's logic."

— PETER DRUCKER

CHAPTER 10

ASSESSING ENTERPRISE READINESS

B y now I hope you're convinced that blockchain is a foundational technology that will transform healthcare.

Where Did We Travel?

Chapter 1 began with our discussion about why blockchain was created and how it works. We also covered the four principles of a permissionless blockchain: distributed, public, time-stamped, and persistent. Blockchain technology isn't only about the tech; it's mostly about the adaptation of new business models specifically around platforms of value. These platforms combine different pieces of infrastructure and base protocols, middleware and services, and applications and solutions to create new value.

We explored how the adoption of new technology often happens in small pieces that appear unconnected. However, these pieces, either months or many years later, reassemble into a new design offering a solution to a new problem—designed from micro-innovations we had the whole time. Television, radio, transportation, computers, space exploration, and medicine have new breakthroughs every day—most of which we, as consumers, will never hear about. That doesn't mean, however, they're any less significant.

The hype associated with new products, services, and interactions is often overemphasized when it shouldn't be. Whether you're considering blockchain technologies, microservices, or virtual reality, start by assessing its relationships to the hype cycle:

1. Innovation trigger
2. Peak of inflated expectations
3. Trough of disillusionment
4. Slope of enlightenment
5. The plateau of productivity

There are no standards, only guidelines to assure the innovation trigger isn't too early and the plateau of productivity isn't too late. Like most things in life, it depends. You, as a healthcare leader, need to make that call.

Chapter 2 answered the questions of "Why?" Why is there value in removing the "trusted third-party?" We quickly moved from permissioned and permissionless blockchains to redactable chains. With that base understanding, we added research from MIT on projects that have the potential to change patient-to-provider-to-payer interactions. Is this considered a disruptive practice? Probably. However, much of the impact or raw disruption will depend on the implementation as well as how existing interactions change between stakeholders within the healthcare ecosystem.

Chapter 3 led us to explore the wonder of Legos and why innovation happens so slowly. Quickly we started to venture into the world of IBM Blockchain on Bluemix with the Starter Developer and High-Security Business Network solution. While you're likely not a developer today, this level of understanding will help you better envision how to align your teams and organizations to leverage this new capability.

Hyperledger is building the fabric for future blockchain capabilities. Even if you don't use IBM technology, understanding its product growth path and approach will provide insights into how to design for value.

Chapter 4 jumped quickly into the Microsoft Bletchley solution and the Ethereum blockchain as a service on Azure.

The business demand for client-driver performance and flexibility makes these offerings very interesting.

We're experiencing a paradigm shift. Years ago, it was most important to buy, build, or lease a complete solution. This solution did everything we could afford to buy. However, that dependency on single vendors quickly became a choke point on innovation and growth. It was so restrictive that we looked for other options. Today, solutions aren't designed around single-vendor offerings. These modern solutions are collages of products and services that, together, uniformly offer increased durability for your business operations. Wait—doesn't more vendors mean more risk? It could. However, in this example we're speaking specifically about increasing the durability of technology capabilities to improve the robustness of business capabilities. By ensuring the foundation is stable, we can be more agile on the surface. It takes a minute to digest, but it makes sense.

We also introduced the idea behind cryptlets—adding a security blockchain middleware. Identity and certificate services, encryption services, cryptlet services, blockchain gateway services, data services, and management and operations collective form the Microsoft blockchain solution.

From here, we opened the door on mobile or Dapps—distributed applications—that run connected to a blockchain technology foundation.

Chapter 5 was all about interoperability. We redefined trust and included how patients, providers, profiles, and access would work in harmony to construct a better patient experience—ultimately a safer patient experience—and we highlighted the conditional privacy challenge Diane had in accessing her electronic medical records.

Chapter 6 looked at government interaction with blockchain in healthcare in the United States. And I gave the term interoperability a fresh definition:

"Healthcare interoperability is the ability of multiple health-care ecosystems to work in harmony without unreasonable efforts by the ecosystems' producers and consumers."

HL7 and FHIR were hot through this chapter, as these technologies hold big opportunities for improving identity matching and trust within the patient experience. We introduced the interoperability framework extracted from the paper "Micro-Identities Improve Healthcare Interoperability with Blockchain."

Chapter 7 was revolutionary. The concept of IPFS enables the Internet of Data Structures (IoDS) to become a reality. Permissioned versus permissionless. On-chain verse off-chain. These are daily struggles when designing blockchain solutions.

However, by using a P2P-like network to store information off-chain, we find the web is no longer a temporary end-point for information. The web evolves into a network of data that now can be transformed into information that can be leveraged to create knowledge that eventually makes its way to wisdom (offering insights previously unknown). The movement from HTTP to IPFS is going to be a slow journey. Yet, like the Internet, it's going to happen.

Chapter 8 was a bit more fun with some practical examples of why it's difficult to find good use cases. Why is it hard to find these use cases? The great innovators and entrepreneurs have already created businesses around them. This results in the encapsulation of those ideas, effectively protecting them from outside eyes looking in—eyes like ours, interested in what business problems they're solving and how the technology is leveraged to address root causes. We did cover a handful of use cases including:

1. Population health management
2. Mobile communications and notification
3. Wearables
4. Patient-generated health data

5. Personal health banks
6. Autonomous monitoring of ubiquitous medical devices
7. Device-to-device sharing of medical information
8. Monitoring devices
9. Teleradiology
10. Immutable patient images
11. Smart health contracts
12. Decentralized applications for health
13. Universal ledger for global genomic sequencing
14. Peer-to-Peer (P2P) insurance
15. Quantified Self-Data Standards
16. Provenance
17. Medical record chain-of-custody
18. Tokenization of health-based services
19. Personal medical record transparency (access to records)
20. Patient interaction with state channels
21. Lightning network off-chain micro-payment (payer and provider)
22. Zero-knowledge, proof-smart contract for a private patient experience

Chapter 9 took a closer look at how healthcare is changing and where change is occurring. It's still amazing to me that, at the Yale Healthcare Hackathon, in under two days and with with minimal funding, so many people got together to make a difference with the goal of improving the patient experience. This is proof positive that not all innovation is expensive or takes years. Sometimes, innovation can occur by just mixing up players to better understand the problems you're trying to solve.

Radbit solved the problem of lost CT scans and x-ray CDs. Rx4All solved the problem of millions in drugs being wasted due to drugs nearing expiration. PAT (Pediatric Assistive Toy) solved every children's fear of going to hospitals: making the experience less scary with a stuffy and furry friend.

These stories impact people. Not just any people but Moms, Dads, sisters, brothers, grandfathers, grandmothers, aunts, and uncles—people we love and care about. This is why understanding technologies and business capabilities, that have the potential to enable health and find better cures, is vital. It's not sort of important. It's everything.

How Innovative Is Your Company?

By now you believe. You understand what blockchain is, how it impacts business, and the effect it could have on our healthcare system. Will every suggestion materialize within the next twelve months? I doubt it. But I do believe a resolution is occurring. It's just happening quietly.

The intent of this book was to outline applications and define the possibilities that surround blockchain. I intentionally didn't explain every technical detail. For the most part, they don't matter. What matters is how healthcare is impacted. As you assess your firm and your company's capabilities to explore blockchain technologies, keep the following five questions in mind:

1. IS YOUR ORGANIZATION CULTURALLY READY?

All too quickly, we race toward the coolest and sexiest technologies. As leaders, we already have to address legacy technologies that impact our ability to deliver value. Blockchain doesn't solve this—not much does. These large modernization efforts are critical to future business sustainability. Removing intermediaries from banks and financial institutions introduces disruption. In a similar way, disruption is injected into the healthcare supply chain.

It's not going to be faster to use blockchain technology. It's going to be slower, at least at first. Have you ever transitioned to a new technology platform? Have you launched a new business process for operations? These initiatives can be summed up in one word: ugly. They're not pretty, and they consume time the team and organization frankly doesn't have. When you're balancing the value of blockchain (and I do think it has monumental value), make sure you confirm that your team and organization is ready. In doing so, consider the following:

- Does the organization handle change well?
- Are processes in place to evaluate new technology for business transformation?
- Is there a strategy roadmap for innovation? How does blockchain fit into that mix?

2. WHERE IS THE SINGLE SOURCE OF TRUTH?

Every initiative has one thing in common, whether we're talking about introducing a simple business-owned application (BOA) for business pricing that's sitting on a colleague's desk or a network of claims systems assembled by 15 mergers over 14 years. That one thing is trust.

Many times, we introduce new components because we know they add value. However, as leaders, we fail to fully evaluate the runway to get that technology business to be effective—that is, to the point where it's adding value to the business.

What we're actually talking about isn't the single source of truth, since that would imply absolute truth or fact. What we're hinting at is a mutually agreed upon version of record. A single place. Blockchain doesn't solve this. It would be nice if it did, but it doesn't. Blockchain technologies don't guarantee authenticity. They can guarantee that each of the 14 systems has been changed but they don't determine which system is authentic and which is not. Why is this relevant? Just putting information on the blockchain doesn't make it easy. In fact, it's inconvenient to access information in a blockchain. It's even more inconvenient to access data your business partners put on the blockchain. Of course, this can be done, and, eventually, I believe it will be a best practice. However, for today, it requires establishing new contracts, business agreements, and SLAs with anyone with whom you exchange data. For many of our organizations, that's a big ask.

- Where's the source system?
- Who owns the source system?
- How are changes made?

3. CAN YOU PILOT OR BUILD AN MVP SAFELY?

Every business book today proclaims it's great to fail and that failing often is welcomed. I hope I'm not the first to share that failing, at any level, when presenting to your Board of Directors, is an uncomfortable and awkward discussion. It also doesn't get easier with time. Over time, your peers on the executive team and the board trust you more. The result is that the discussion gets worse, not better.

The conversation therefore needs to change. It shouldn't be about trying things with the hope maybe something will work. The odds say that likely nothing will work and, months later, that great presentation you gave about innovation will result in, well, not much innovation.

I'd propose an alternative. Start with the premise that you plan to fail. In fact, this entire exercise has no desire to win. It's a learning experience for your team. You're increasing your understanding of a progressive technology and, collectively, the team is going to work with one business partner or customer to build a minimally viable product together. The goal, unofficially, is to create nothing and, officially, to build a better relationship with that partner or client.

It's hard to create things. It's even harder to create things that work and that people are willing to pay for. Setting your team up for success means communicating from the start that the plan is only to learn—nothing more, nothing less. Consider it part of training or education or ongoing career development—whatever you think you can sell. But the net outcome is that your team or organization is going to increase its capability in this space, which may lead to improving some to-be-determined future project.

This MVP must be aligned to a partner or customer; it can't be done in an internal silo. Give your team exposure to venture out and build a new relationship.

- Have you establishing a partner or customer for the MVP?
- Are your peers and other members of the executive team on board with this experiment as an exercise to build better relationships (with no other outcome expected)?
- Do you, as a leader, have the time to dedicate to this initiative (MVP) to ensure partner and customer relationships grow and don't decline?

4. HAVE YOU ENGAGED A BLOCKCHAIN LEADER AND EXPERT TO ADVISE YOU?

You can learn to ride a bike on your own, and it's possible to pick up skiing by watching TV, though neither are recommended.

Change is a different beast. Why is it that we're superior planners and inferior doers? If you go back through your email, there's probably a package of business roadmap documents charting the way to champagne dinners and caviar dreams. Of course, no one reads them. No one refers to them. But we have them, so check off that box! This is where a partner plays a role. We all need someone to keep us accountable.

Engaging a trusted partner can help ensure you don't ride your bike into a ditch or ski off the trail.

- Have you identified a trusted partner?
- Is there a knowledgeable and industry-respected expert you can engage to validate your approach regarding blockchain?

- Are you open to opinions that might suggest a current approach needs to be adjusted and that you'll have to communicate that throughout the organization?

5. HAVE YOU DESIGNED A COMMUNITY FOR ACCELERATING IDEAS?

We hear a lot about innovation towers within companies. And sometimes there's an innovation group, team, or special something where "innovation" is supposed to happen.

Those of us who've been designing teams and delivering transformative and innovative solutions know this rarely works. Innovation and, ultimately, the adoption of new technology has very little to do with the technology—it has everything to do with the people. If the technology sucks but the people are on board, you have a shot at success. However, if the technology is amazing and the organization doesn't buy in, there's no hope for acceptance of that technology into business operations. Obviously, we hope the technology is great and the company embraces the idea.

So, now that you're at the end of the book, I have a secret. The technology isn't going to transform anything without people. Your people must care enough to accept change and understand how these benefits can improve the patient experience and save lives. We, as leaders, can design systems, orchestrate interactions, and incentivize behaviors. This is the stuff we do. However, for every conversation you have about technology, you should also have five conversations on culture and people.

- Have you established an internal network of teams to support innovation?
- Is there a formal process to manage how change happens in the organization, which measures its effect on people (morale, behavior etc.)? Prioritization meetings don't count.
- Do you believe blockchain has value, and can you effectively communicate that to your mother?

If you've read these questions and feel confident you and your organization are ready, excellent!

We do this to create change and deliver innovative concepts that have the potential to transform the world. It's why we all care. More importantly, it's why we believe.

Blockchain Competencies

What skills do you feel best prepare you for improving your ability to thrive with blockchain technology?

Functional:
- ☐ Industry, Domain, and Client Knowledge
- ☐ Business Acumen
- ☐ Platform Economics
- ☐ Blockchain Business, and Operating Models
- ☐ Market Offerings e.g., Blockchain as a Service (BaaS)
- ☐ Principles of Cryptography
- ☐ Large Datasets
- ☐ Knowledge of Bitcoin, Ethereum, and Hyperledger
- ☐ Distributed Applications (Dapps) Utility

Technical:
- ☐ Distributed and Service Architectures
- ☐ Blockchain Types and Utility
- ☐ Business and Technical System Design
- ☐ Provider and Hosting Market e.g., IBM Blockchain and Microsoft Azure Blockchain
- ☐ Programming Smart Contracts: Solidity, LLL, Serpent, JAVA, C++, Golang, Node.js, and Python

Core:
- ☐ Relationship Management
- ☐ Integrity
- ☐ Personal Accountability
- ☐ Business SME (Finance, Healthcare, or Energy etc.)
- ☐ Learning Intelligence (Ability to Learn)

Building Individual Blockchain Intelligence

How strong is your understanding of blockchain technologies and its potential to impact your healthcare business?

For each of the three questions, rate yourself using a scale from 1 to 5, where 1 = strongly disagree; 3 = neutral; and 5 = strongly agree, and find the recommended action for your score.

Are you building the essential capabilities for blockchain intelligence?	Score
Can you the describe the value of DLT?	
Are you familiar with how individual transactions (blocks) are added to a digital ledger (chain)?	
Do you understand the benefits and risks associated with distributed infrastructures?	
Can you articulate how your products, services, and interactions would fit into a blockchain-enabled world?	
Have you established a network of blockchain advisors or experts?	
	Total Score

SCORING

Over 22: You have the foundational capabilities you need for improving your understanding of blockchain technologies; 12-22: You've started to implement changes to improve your blockchain technology knowledge but more is needed; Less than 12: You need to consider specific actions to improve your foundational understanding of blockchain technology.

Growing Team Blockchain Intelligence

How well is your team developing its blockchain technology capabilities?

For each of the three questions, rate your team or organization using a scale from 1 to 5, where 1 = strongly disagree; 3 = neutral; and 5 = strongly agree, and find the recommended action for your score.

Is your organization building the essential capabilities for blockchain intelligence?	Score
Have you clearly defined how your industry may be impacted by blockchain technologies?	
Does executive leadership understand the benefit and risks associated with DLT?	
Is innovation a defined process and not an event within your organization?	
Is the team realistically capable of supporting more foundational change?	
Is blockchain technology part of a larger strategic approach for growth?	
Total Score	

SCORING

Over 22: Your team has the foundational capabilities required for improving their understanding of blockchain technologies; 12-22: Your team has started to implement changes to improve their knowledge of blockchain technologies; Less than 12: Your team needs to consider specific actions to improve the team's foundational awareness of blockchain technologies.

Assessing Team Capabilities to Drive Blockchain

How well is your team staffed to ensure the right mix of blockchain resources?

For each of the five questions, rate your team using a scale from 1 to 5, where 1 = strongly disagree; 3 = neutral, and 5 = strongly agree, and find the recommended action for your score.

Is your team staffed correctly to ensure a successful pilot or MVP?	Score
Data: Does the team have data and analytics staff who understand distributed data storage models?	
Compute: Have infrastructure teams established consensus algorithms, compute nodes, communication protocols, or equivalents?	
Develop: Is the team familiar with contract development languages, inter-ledger communications, smart contracts, oracles, and explores for chain data"	
Lead: Are the technology and business leaders familiar with deploying blockchain technologies?	
	Total Score

SCORING

Over 17: Your team has the foundational capabilities required to successful deploy an MVP or pilot with blockchain technologies; **10-17:** Your team has started to acquire the skills to implement blockchain technologies but more education is needed; **Less than 10:** you need to reconsider whether your team is honestly positioned for success. Outside help may be an option.

The 21 Irrefutable Laws of Blockchains

Are you curious how to evaluate products, services, and interactions that involve distributed ledger technologies?

These 21 principles combine insights and observations from the world of blockchain.

1. The Law of Value
2. The Law of Others
3. The Law of Intermediation
4. The Law of Exchange
5. The Law of Reward
6. The Law of Use
7. The Law of Proof
8. The Law of Consensus
9. The Law of Acceleration
10. The Law of Trust
11. The Law of Diffusion
12. The Law of Participation
13. The Law of Repudiation
14. The Law of Replication
15. The Law of Fees
16. The Law of Immutabilities
17. The Law of Autonomy
18. The Law of Decentralization
19. The Law of Relevance
20. The Law of Vulnerabilities
21. The Law of Incentives

Additional information can be found at:

www.leadersneedpancakes.com/blockchainbook

PUBLISHED PAPER 1

Citation:
Nichol, P. B., & Brandt, J. (2016). Co-Creation of Trust for Healthcare: The Cryptocitizen Framework for Interoperability with Blockchain, 9. http://doi.org/10.13140/RG.2.1.1545.4963

Abstract
The aim of this paper is to integrate the concept of co-creation of trust for healthcare and propose applications of blockchain to positively impact aspects of healthcare interoperability. The focus of the paper is on blockchain health ecosystems and the patient-centered interactions that underpin the co-creation of trust, balancing the pluralistic morality of identity. The co-creation of trust in the healthcare framework is divided into four concepts applied to healthcare based on the underlying theoretical foundation. Blockchain is a database and technology that facilitates an exchange of value within a trust-less network, without intermediaries. These conceptualized propositions suggest that co-creation of trust ecosystems has a direct positive impact on patient satisfaction, fraud, healthcare outcomes, and reduces the security risks associated with interoperability. This paper contributes to the literature on co-creation of trust within healthcare ecosystems leveraging blockchain.

PUBLISHED PAPER 2

Citation:
Nichol, P. B., & Dailey, MD, W. R. (2016). Micro-Identities Improve Healthcare Interoperability with Blockchain: Deterministic Methods for Connecting Patient Data to Uniform Patient Identifiers, 10. http://doi.org/10.13140/RG.2.1.3118.3605

Abstract
The aim of this paper is to present solutions to the ongoing concerns about healthcare interoperability within the United States. Technological changes promise to improve healthcare. Provider-to-provider data transfers within a trustless ecosystem is possible by leveraging blockchain technologies. Blockchain has the potential to enable healthcare interoperability alignment to address identity, confidentiality, integrity of data, and accessibility. This paper presents a hybrid model, integrating HL7 FHIR interoperability standards describing data formats and elements as well as an Application Programming Interface (API) for exchanging electronic health records using blockchain technologies for better patient access to health information. This research expands traditional identity-matching strategies to formulate a new solution for healthcare entities to match patient identities. This paper contributes to the literature on the potential for blockchain technologies as they relate to improving the patient care continuum, thus empowering patient self-sovereignty.

PUBLISHED PAPER 3

Citation
Nichol, P. B. (2017). An e-Government Interoperability Framework to Reduce Waste, Fraud, and Abuse, 11. http://doi.org/10.13140/RG.2.2.18000.51209.

Abstract
The aim of this paper is to present a practical approach for separate entities to share information within the United States through an e-Government Interoperability Framework. Waste, fraud, and abuse have increased year-over-year in Medicare, Medicaid, and the Children's Health Insurance Program (CHIP). Interoperability frameworks based on a foundation of digital ledger technologies have the potential to connect disparate information systems. This paper presents an Interoperability Framework to connect the public and private sector together with minimal impact to legacy federal, state, and private information systems. The Interoperability Framework is a distributed (no central operator), heterogeneous (connects systems on any platform), and secure (ensures authenticity, integrity, and non-repudiation of exchanged data) approach to an inter-organizational data exchange framework without changing the ownership or location of data.

CITING THE BOOK

APA

Nichol, P. B. (2017). The Power of Blockchain for Healthcare: How Blockchain Will Ignite The Future of Healthcare (1st ed.). Newington, CT USA: OROCA Innovations.

CHICAGO

Nichol, Peter B. The Power of Blockchain for Healthcare: How Blockchain Will Ignite The Future of Healthcare. 1st ed. Newington, CT USA: OROCA Innovations, 2017.

ELSEVIER HARVARD

Nichol, P.B., 2017. The Power of Blockchain for Healthcare: How Blockchain Will Ignite The Future of Healthcare, 1st ed. OROCA Innovations, Newington, CT USA.

IEEE

P. B. Nichol, The Power of Blockchain for Healthcare: How Blockchain Will Ignite The Future of Healthcare, 1st ed. Newington, CT USA: OROCA Innovations, 2017.

NOTES

CHAPTER 1. INTRODUCTION

1. Nakamoto, S. (2008). Bitcoin: A Peer-to-Peer Electronic Cash System. Retrieved from https://bitcoin.org/bitcoin.pdf

2. Nichol, P. B., & Brandt, J. (2016). Co-Creation of Trust for Healthcare: The Cryptocitizen Framework for Interoperability with Blockchain, 9. http://doi.org/10.13140/RG.2.1.1545.4963

3. Ibid.

4. CNN, M. M. (2015). Officials respond to Haiti Red Cross scandal. Retrieved April 2, 2017, http://www.cnn.com/2015/06/04/americas/american-red-cross-haiti-controversy-propublica-npr/

5. Association of Certified Fraud Examiners, Inc. (2016). 2016 ACFE Report to the Nations. Retrieved April 2, 2017, from http://www.acfe.com/rttn

6. Minitab, Inc. (2016). Weather Forecasts: Just How Reliable Are They? Retrieved April 2, 2017, from http://www.minitab.com/en-us/Published-Articles/Weather-Forecasts--Just-How-Reliable-Are-They-/

7. Niles, R. (n.d.). Standard Deviation. Retrieved April 2, 2017, from http://www.robertniles.com/stats/stdev.shtml

8. S&P Capital IQ. (2017). Verizon Communications: Company Profile.

9. Statista. (2016). Global smartphones sales revenue 2013-2016. Retrieved April 3, 2017, from https://www.statista.com/statistics/237505/global-revenue-from-smartphones-since-2008/

10. NASA. (n.d.). NASA - NSSDCA - Spacecraft - Luna 2. Retrieved April 2, 2017, from https://nssdc.gsfc.nasa.gov/nmc/spacecraftDisplay.do?id=1959-014A

11. NASA. (n.d.). NASA - NSSDCA - Spacecraft - Luna 3. Retrieved April 2, 2017, from https://nssdc.gsfc.nasa.gov/nmc/spacecraftDisplay.do?id=1959-008A

12. NASA. (n.d.). Ranger 7. Retrieved April 2, 2017, from http://www.jpl.nasa.gov/missions/ranger-7/

13. NASA. (n.d.). Ranger 8. Retrieved April 2, 2017, from http://www.jpl.nasa.gov/missions/ranger-8/

14. Columbia University Medical Center. (2017). Brief History of Heart Transplantation. Retrieved April 2, 2017, from http://columbiasurgery.org/heart-transplant/brief-history-heart-transplantation

15. Cuomo, J. (2016). IBMVoice: Blockchain: The Foundation For The Future Of Transactions. Retrieved April 2, 2017, from http://www.forbes.com/sites/ibm/2016/02/17/blockchain-the-foundation-for-the-future-of-transactions/

16. Webb, A. (2015). The Tech Trends You Can't Ignore in 2015. Retrieved April 2, 2017, from https://hbr.org/2015/01/the-tech-trends-you-cant-ignore-in-2015

17. Cortese, A. (2016). Blockchain technology ushers in the "Internet of Value." Retrieved April 2, 2017, from https://newsroom.cisco.com/feature-content?type=webcontent&articleId=1741667

18. Kastelein, R. (2016). PwC launches New Global Technology Team to Tap into Blockchain. Retrieved from http://www.the-blockchain.com/2016/04/04/pwc-launches-new-global-technology-team-to-tap-into-blockchain/

19. Deloitte. (2016). Blockchain: Enigma. Paradox. Opportunity. Retrieved from https://www2.deloitte.com/content/dam/Deloitte/nl/Documents/financial-services/deloitte-nl-fsi-blockchain-enigma-paradox-opportunity-report.pdf

20. Coindesk. (2017). Bitcoin Venture Capital Funding. Retrieved April 3, 2017, from http://www.coindesk.com/bitcoin-venture-capital/

21. Fenn, J., & Raskino, M. (2008). Mastering the Hype Cycle: How to Choose the Right Innovation at the Right Time. Boston, Mass: Harvard Business Review Press.

CHAPTER 2. IDEAS THAT BEND CONVENTION

1. Collins, M. (2015). The Big Bank Bailout. Retrieved April 2, 2017, from http://www.forbes.com/sites/mikecollins/2015/07/14/the-big-bank-bailout/

2. Corkery, M. (2016). Elizabeth Warren Accuses Wells Fargo Chief of "Gutless Leadership." Retrieved April 2, 2017, from https://www.nytimes.com/2016/09/21/business/dealbook/wells-fargo-ceo-john-stumpf-senate-testimony.html

3. Ateniese, G., Magri, B., Venturi, D., & Andrade, E. (2016). Redactable Blockchain, or Rewriting History in Bitcoin and Friends (p. 38). Retrieved from http://eprint.iacr.org/2016/757.pdf

4. Krawczyk, H., & Rabin, T. (n.d.). Chameleon Signature (p. 12). Retrieved from http://www.internetsociety.org/sites/default/files/Chameleon%20Signatures%20(paper)%20(Hugo%20Krawczyk).pdf

5. Chaum D. (1991) Zero-Knowledge Undeniable Signatures (extended abstract). In: Damgård I.B. (eds) Advances in Cryptology — EUROCRYPT '90. EUROCRYPT 1990. Lecture Notes in Computer Science, vol 473. Springer, Berlin, Heidelberg

6. Bos, J. N.E. (1992). Practical Privacy (p. 127). Retrieved from http://alexandria.tue.nl/repository/books/369616.pdf

7. Bos, J.N.E., & Chaum D. (1993) Provably Unforgeable Signatures. In: Brickell E.F. (eds) Advances in Cryptology — CRYPTO' 92. CRYPTO 1992. Lecture Notes in Computer Science, vol 740. Springer, Berlin, Heidelberg

8. Accenture. (2016). Editing the Uneditable blockchain: Why distributed ledger technology must adapt to an imperfect world (p. 8). Retrieved from http://newsroom.accenture.com/content/1101/files/Cross-FSBC.pdf

9. Ateniese, G., Magri, B., Venturi, D., & Andrade, E. (2016). Redactable Blockchain or Rewriting History in Bitcoin and Friends (p. 38). Retrieved from http://eprint.iacr.org/2016/757.pdf

10. Blockchain Luxembourg S. A. (2017). Total Number of Transactions. Retrieved April 3, 2017, from https://blockchain.info/n-transactions-total

11. MIT Sloan School of Management. (2016). How Blockchain Will Transform the Digital Economy. Retrieved April 2, 2017, from https://www.youtube.com/watch?v=kaq0bwTuu1Q

12. Hernández, J. C. (2016). China Censors WeChat Rumors, Including the One About Robots Taking Over. Retrieved April 2, 2017, from https://www.nytimes.com/2016/06/25/world/what-in-the-world/china-wechat-censor-rumors.html

13. Venkataraman, A. (2016). India Film Censor Orders 94 Cuts to Movie About Punjab's Drug Problem. Retrieved April 2, 2017, from https://www.nytimes.com/2016/06/10/world/asia/india-film-censor-orders-94-cuts-to-movie-about-punjabs-drug-problem.html

14. Artstor Blog. (2013). Michelangelo's Last Judgment—uncensored. Retrieved from https://artstor.wordpress.com/2013/11/13/michelangelos-last-judgment-uncensored/

15. W3C. (2016). W3C Blockchains and the Web Workshop. Retrieved April 2, 2017, from https://www.w3.org/2016/04/blockchain-workshop/#position-statements

16. W3C. (2016). Information needed to answer Blockchains and the Web Workshop Expression of Interest - Web-Based Straw-poll and Balloting System. Retrieved April 2, 2017, from https://www.w3.org/2002/09/wbs/1/blockchain-workshop/

17. Narayanan, A. (2017). Arvind Narayanan. Retrieved April 2, 2017, from https://freedom-to-tinker.com/author/randomwalker/

18. Narayanan, A. (2017). 33 Bits of Entropy. Retrieved April 2, 2017, from https://33bits.org/

19. Coursera. (2017). Bitcoin and Cryptocurrency Technologies - Princeton University. Retrieved April 2, 2017, from https://www.coursera.org/learn/cryptocurrency

20. Narayanan, A., Bonneau, J., Felten, E., Miller, A., & Goldfeder, S. (2016). Bitcoin and Cryptocurrency Technologies. Retrieved from https://d28rh4a8wq0iu5.cloudfront.net/bitcointech/readings/princeton_bitcoin_book.pdf

21. Duranti, L., & MacNeil, H. (1996). The Protection of the Integrity of Electronic Records: An Overview for the UBC-MAS Research Project. Retrieved from http://archivaria.ca/index.php/archivaria/article/download/12153/13158

22. Zyskind, G., Nathan, O., & Pentland, A. (2015). Enigma: Decentralized Computation Platform withGuaranteed Privacy (p. 2). Retrieved from http://www.enigma.co/enigma_full.pdf

23. Montjoye, Y.-A. de, Shmueli, E., Wang, S. S., & Pentland, A. S. (2014). openPDS: Protecting the Privacy of Metadata through SafeAnswers. PLOS ONE, 9(7), 1. https://doi.org/10.1371/journal.pone.0098790

CHAPTER 3. IBM'S BLOCKCHAIN SOLUTION

1. IBM. (2016). IBM Launches Blockchain Cloud on World's Most Secure Server [CTB10]. Retrieved April 3, 2017, from https://www-03.ibm.com/press/us/en/pressrelease/50169.wss

2. IBM. (2017). IBM LinuxONE. Retrieved April 3, 2017, from https://www.ibm.com/systems/linuxone/

3. IBM. (2013). Testing consensus and availability. Retrieved April 3, 2017, from https://console.ng.bluemix.net/docs/services/blockchain/etn_pbft.html

4. IBM. (2016). Blockchain - IBM Bluemix. Retrieved April 3, 2017, from https://console.ng.bluemix.net/catalog/services/blockchain/

5. IBM. (2017). IBM-Blockchain/marbles. Retrieved April 3, 2017, from https://github.com/IBM-Blockchain/marbles

6. IBM. (2016). IBM-Blockchain/cp-web. Retrieved April 3, 2017, from https://github.com/IBM-Blockchain/cp-web

7. IBM. (2016). IBM-Blockchain/car-lease-demo. Retrieved April 3, 2017, from https://github.com/IBM-Blockchain/car-lease-demo

8. IBM. (2016). ITPeople-Blockchain/auction. Retrieved April 3, 2017, from https://github.com/ITPeople-Blockchain/auction

9. IBM. (2016). Healthcare rallies for blockchains: Keeping patients at the center (p. 24). Retrieved from https://public.dhe.ibm.com/common/ssi/ecm/gb/en/gbe03790usen/GBE03790USEN.PDF

10. Kleinrock, L. (2014). Leonard Kleinrock's Home Page. Retrieved April 3, 2017, from https://www.lk.cs.ucla.edu/index.html

11. Ripple. (2017). ripple/rippled. Retrieved April 3, 2017, from https://github.com/ripple/rippled

12. Hyperledger. (2017). hyperledger/hyperledger. Retrieved April 3, 2017, from https://github.com/hyperledger/hyperledger

13. Digital Asset Holdings. (2017). DigitalAssetCom/hlp-candidate. Retrieved April 3, 2017, from https://github.com/DigitalAssetCom/hlp-candidate

14. Elements Project. (2017). The Elements Project. Retrieved April 3, 2017, from https://elementsproject.org/

CHAPTER 4. MICROSOFT'S BLOCKCHAIN SOLUTION

1. Microsoft. (2016). Introducing Project Bletchley and elements of blockchain born in the Microsoft Cloud. Retrieved April 3, 2017, from https://azure.microsoft.com/en-us/blog/bletchley-blockchain/

2. Microsoft. (2017). Azure/azure-blockchain-projects. Retrieved April 3, 2017, from https://github.com/Azure/azure-blockchain-projects

3. Microsoft. (2015). Ethereum Blockchain as a Service now on Azure. Retrieved April 3, 2017, from https://azure.microsoft.com/en-us/blog/ethereum-blockchain-as-a-service-now-on-azure/

4. ConsenSys Media. (2017). Ethereum. Retrieved April 3, 2017, from https://consensys.net

5. Mandeleil, R. (2017). Ether.Camp. Retrieved April 3, 2017, from https://github.com/ether-camp

6. Starkey, A. (n.d.). Try BlockApps to quickly build, scale and deploy blockchain applications. Retrieved April 3, 2017, from http://blockapps.net/

CHAPTER 5. REFRAMING HEALTHCARE INTEROPERABILITY

1. Economist. (2015). The promise of the blockchain: The trust machine. Retrieved November 16, 2015, from http://www.economist.com/news/leaders/21677198-technology-behind-bitcoin-could-transform-how-economy-works-trust-machine

2. Mougayar, W. (2015). Understanding the blockchain - O'Reilly Radar. Retrieved November 16, 2015, from http://radar.oreilly.com/2015/01/understanding-the-blockchain.html

3. Williams, R. (2015). How Bitcoin Tech Could Make Supply Chains More Transparent. Retrieved April 3, 2017, from http://www.coindesk.com/how-bitcoins-technology-could-make-supply-chains-more-transparent/

CHAPTER 6. PLAYING WITH GOVERNMENTS

1. Nichol, P. B., & Dailey, MD, W. R. (2016). Micro-Identities Improve Healthcare Interoperability with Blockchain: Deterministic Methods for Connecting Patient Data to Uniform Patient Identifiers, 10. http://doi.org/10.13140/RG.2.1.3118.3605

2. Interview with Gil Alterovitz.

3. Nichol, P. B., & Dailey, MD, W. R. (2016). Micro-Identities Improve Healthcare Interoperability with Blockchain: Deterministic Methods for Connecting Patient Data to Uniform Patient Identifiers, 10. http://doi.org/10.13140/RG.2.1.3118.3605

4. Nichol, P. B., & Brandt, J. (2016). Co-Creation of Trust for Healthcare: The Cryptocitizen Framework for Interoperability with Blockchain, 9. http://doi.org/10.13140/RG.2.1.1545.4963

5. Ibid.

6. Ibid.

7. Nichol, P. B., & Dailey, MD, W. R. (2016). Micro-Identities Improve Healthcare Interoperability with Blockchain: Deterministic Methods for Connecting Patient Data to Uniform Patient Identifiers, 10. http://doi.org/10.13140/RG.2.1.3118.3605

8. Ibid.

9. Ibid.

10. Interview with Wayne Kubick.

11. Nichol, P. B., & Dailey, MD, W. R. (2016). Micro-Identities Improve Healthcare Interoperability with Blockchain: Deterministic Methods for Connecting Patient Data to Uniform Patient Identifiers, 10. http://doi.org/10.13140/RG.2.1.3118.3605

CHAPTER 7. THE DISTRIBUTED WEB: IPFS

1. Benet, J. (2014). IPFS - Content Addressed, Versioned, P2P File System (DRAFT 3). Retrieved from https://ipfs.io/ipfs/Qm-R7GSQM93Cx5eAg6a6yRzNde1FQv7uL6X1o4k7zrJa3LX/ipfs.draft3.pdf

2. Free Software Foundation. (2017). GNU General Public License. Retrieved April 3, 2017, from https://www.gnu.org/licenses/gpl-3.0.en.html

3. IPFS. (2017). IPFS is the Distributed Web. Retrieved April 3, 2017, from https://ipfs.io/

4. IPNS. (2017). ipfs/examples. Retrieved April 3, 2017, from https://github.com/ipfs/examples

5. IPLD. (2017). ipld/specs. Retrieved April 3, 2017, from https://github.com/ipld/specs

6. LIBP2P. (2017). libp2p. Retrieved April 3, 2017, from https://github.com/libp2p

7. Mazieres, D., Kaminsky, M., Kaashoek, M. F., & Witchel, E. (1999). Separating key management from files system security. In Operating Systems Review (34(5), pp. 124–139). Retrieved from https://pdos.csail.mit.edu/papers/sfs:sosp99.pdf

8. Nichol, P. B. (2017). An e-Government Interoperability Framework to Reduce Waste, Fraud, and Abuse, 11. http://doi.org/10.13140/RG.2.2.18000.51209.

9. Chainthat. (n.d.). Blockchain Basics Explained - Hashes with Mining and Merkle trees. 2016. Retrieved from https://www.youtube.com/watch?v=lik9aaFIsl4

10. Bertoni G., Daemen J., Peeters M., Van Assche G. (2014) Sakura: A Flexible Coding for Tree Hashing. In: Boureanu I., Owesarski P., Vaudenay S. (eds) Applied Cryptography and Network Security. ACNS 2014. Lecture Notes in Computer Science, vol 8479. Springer, Cham

11. Merkle, R. C. (1979). Secrecy, Authentication, and Public Key Systems (Ph.D. thesis). Stanford University.

CHAPTER 8. PRACTICAL USE CASES

1. Nichol, P. B., & Brandt, J. (2016). Co-Creation of Trust for Healthcare: The Cryptocitizen Framework for Interoperability with Blockchain, 9. http://doi.org/10.13140/RG.2.1.1545.4963

2. Ibid.

3. Nichol, P. B., & Dailey, MD, W. R. (2016). Micro-Identities Improve Healthcare Interoperabil-ity with Blockchain: Deterministic Methods for Connecting Patient Data to Uniform Patient Identifiers, 10. http://doi.org/10.13140/RG.2.1.3118.3605

4. Singh, H., Meyer, A. N. D., & Thomas, E. J. (2014). The frequency of diagnostic errors in outpatient care: estimations from three large observational studies involving US adult populations. BMJ Quality & Safety, 23(9), 727. https://doi.org/10.1136/bmjqs-2013-002627

5. Zwickl, D. J. (2008). GARLI. Retrieved April 3, 2017, from http://www.bio.utexas.edu/faculty/antisense/garli/garli.html

6. West, J. (2012). John West - Canned Tuna Fish & Salmon incl Recipes. Retrieved April 3, 2017, from https://www.john-west.co.uk/

7. Custodio, N. (2013). Explain Bitcoin Like I'm Five – Nik Custodio – Medium. Retrieved April 3, 2017, from https://medium.com/@nik5ter/explain-bitcoin-like-im-five-73b4257ac833

8. Rogers, B. (2016). How the Blockchain Can Change the Music Industry (Part 2). Retrieved from https://medium.com/cuepoint/how-the-blockchain-can-change-the-music-industry-part-2-c1fa3bdfa848

9. Tse, C. (2016). Dotblockchain Concept (Edition 2 of 100). Retrieved April 3, 2017, from https://monegraph.com/m6788760298

10. Insurance Information Institute. (2016). Industry Overview. Retrieved April 4, 2017, from http://www.iii.org/fact-statistic/industry-overview

11. Colemann, J. (2017). State Channels - an explanation. Retrieved April 3, 2017, from http://www.jeffcoleman.ca/state-channels/

12. Bitcoin. (2017). Developer Guide - Bitcoin. Retrieved April 3, 2017, from https://bitcoin.org/en/developer-guide#micropayment-channel

13. Poon, J., & Dryja, T. (2016). The Bitcoin Lightning Network: Scalable Off-Chain Instant Payments. Retrieved from https://lightning.network/lightning-network-paper.pdf

14. Ibid.

15. Goldwasser, S., Micali, S., & Rackoff, C. (1985). The Knowledge Compexity of Interactive Proof-Systems. Retrieved from http://groups.csail.mit.edu/cis/pubs/shafi/1985-stoc.pdf

16. Hohenberger, S. (2007). 600.641 Special Topics in Theoretical Cryptography. Retrieved from http://www.cs.jhu.edu/~susan/600.641/scribes/lecture3.pdf

CHAPTER 9. COMPANIES TO WATCH

1. Neumann, J. von, Morgenstern, O., Kuhn, H. W., & Rubinstein, A. (2007). Theory of Games and Economic Behavior (60th Anniversary Commemorative edition). Princeton, N.J. ; Woodstock: Princeton University Press.

2. Brandenburger, A. M., & Nalebuff, B. (1995). The Right Game: Use Game Theory to Shape Strategy. Retrieved April 3, 2017, from https://hbr.org/1995/07/the-right-game-use-game-theory-to-shape-strategy

INDEX

Recently from OROCA Innovations: Author Peter B. Nichol, an MIT Sloan School of Management-recognized CIO and award-winning innovation leader, explores the forgotten world of learning—the ability to learn—in the book entitled, *Learning Intelligence.*

"*Peter dives into unexplored, valuable territory in Learning Intelligence. A must-read for any leader wanting to compete in the innovation-powered landscape of today.*"

— MARSHALL GOLDSMITH,
THE AUTHOR OF THE #1 NEW YORK TIMES BESTSELLER,
TRIGGERS

Available April 28, 2017
www.LearningIntelligenceBook.com

Made in the USA
Middletown, DE
25 July 2017